Mediation and Arbitration of Employment Disputes

John T. Dunlop

Arnold M. Zack

Mediation
and Arbitration
of Employment
Disputes

Jossey-Bass Publishers • San Francisco

Substantial discounts on bulk quantities of Jossey-Bass books are available to corporations, professional associations, and other organizations. For details and discount information, contact the special sales department at Jossey-Bass Inc., Publishers. (415) 433–1740; Fax (800) 605–2665.

For sales outside the United States, please contact your local Simon & Schuster International Office.

Jossey-Bass Web address: http://www.josseybass.com

 Manufactured in the United States of America on Lyons Falls Turin Book. This paper is acid-free and 100 percent totally chlorine-free.

Library of Congress Cataloging-in-Publication Data

Dunlop, John Thomas, (date)
    Mediation and arbitration of employment disputes / John T. Dunlop, Arnold M. Zack.
        p. cm. — (Jossey-Bass conflict resolution series)
    Includes bibliographical references and index.
    ISBN 0–7879–0847–9
    1. Conflict management. 2. Mediation. 3. Dispute resolution (Law) I. Zack, Arnold. II. Title. III. Series.
HD42.D86 1997
658.4'053—dc21   97-16797
                                                                CIP

FIRST EDITION
HB Printing   10 9 8 7 6 5 4 3 2 1

The Jossey-Bass

Conflict Resolution Series

The Jossey-Bass Conflict Resolution Series addresses the growing need for guidelines in the field of conflict resolution, as broadly defined to include negotiation, mediation, alternative dispute resolution, and other forms of third-party intervention. Our books bridge theory and practice, ranging from descriptive analysis to prescriptive advice. Our goal is to provide those engaged in understanding and finding new and more effective ways to approach conflict—practitioners, researchers, teachers, and those in other professional and volunteer pursuits—with the resources to further their work and better the world in which we live.

This series is dedicated to
the life and work of
Jeffrey Z. Rubin
1941–1995

Contents

Preface

Toward a Fair, Affordable, and Expeditious Procedure for Employment Conflict Resolution

As the new millennium approaches, the nation is falling short of its commitment to provide workers effective access to the protections of the country's employment statutes. In this volume, we aim to encourage the use and development of mediation and arbitration in the adjudication of disputes over employment laws and regulations. Our focus is on the evolution of workplace protections through private and statutory rights and on the advantages and disadvantages of the current procedures for resolving workplace disputes. We propose a course of action for bringing greater access to workplace statutory protection to the 125 million in the nation's workforce.

Over the past century the country has developed two paths to resolve workplace disputes. One has been through the use of collective bargaining, by which employers and union organizations of their workers have negotiated mutually acceptable arrangements over wages, hours, and working conditions. As part of these negotiations virtually all collective bargaining agreements contain procedures for private resolution of disputes related to the provisions of the agreement, which might otherwise tend to disrupt workplace tranquility. The collective bargaining process, the dispute settlement machinery of grievance procedures and arbitration, and the decisions arising from these procedures have been encouraged by labor-management consensus and by statute, and they have been endorsed and enforced by the courts as the established means for resolving employment disputes related to the collective agreement.

The first two chapters of this book examine the evolution of these processes of voluntary dispute resolution through grievance procedures and arbitration and the role of collective bargaining in achieving industrial peace.

The other path for resolving workplace problems has been through ever-expanding statutory protections for employees at their workplace, which allow people to resort to administrative agencies and the courts for enforcement. In the past three decades Congress and the state legislatures have enacted numerous individual workplace protections, including Title Seven of the Civil Rights Act, the Americans with Disabilities Act, the Age Discrimination in Employment Act (ADEA), and other antidiscrimination statutes administered and enforced by the Equal Employment Opportunities Commission (EEOC) and its state counterparts. The Occupational Safety and Health Act (OSHA), the Family and Medical Leave Act, and a number of whistleblower statutes are administered and enforced by the Department of Labor. Chapter Three examines the evolution and status of that enforcement, including the limitations for employees seeking to secure the full exercise of their statutory rights. Experience teaches that the resolution of some disputes under employment law is simplified—if not largely eliminated—when the regulations or rules under the statutes are developed in the authorized process of negotiated rulemaking. This process gives the parties who must live under the laws a voice in the process before the regulations are promulgated. This chapter describes the emergence of administrative agency adjudication of disputes and negotiated rulemaking.

Chapter Four examines the role of the Supreme Court in treating disputes under the two paths of collective bargaining and agency litigation; the *Steelworkers Trilogy*, 1960, proclaimed the values of private grievance arbitration under collective bargaining in resolving workplace disputes, while *Alexander* v. *Gardner-Denver*, 1974, restricted labor-management arbitration in efforts to apply statutory protections to workers under collective bargaining agreements. The 1991 decision of the Court in *Gilmer*

v. *Interstate/Johnson Lane Corp.* changed the employment landscape by empowering an arbitrator under the 1925 Federal Arbitration Act to issue a final and binding award in a case where the employee was held to have waived the right to statutory appeal under the ADEA. While that case may have been narrow in its ruling, it has had the impact of forcing a reexamination of the extent to which private dispute settlement mechanisms can thwart access to statutory and judicial protections in the workplace.

Most courts seem to be in lockstep with the *Gilmer* decision, but the law is unsettled and there remain serious questions as to the future of workplace dispute resolution. It is not yet clear whether *Gilmer* constitutes a merging of the two earlier courses of our employment dispute settlement history by encouraging private arbitration of statutory employment issues traditionally considered to be the province of the statutory regulatory agencies.

Although the *Gilmer* decision was confined to arbitration of an ADEA claim that arose under a structure dedicated to registration matters within the securities industry, it triggered numerous employer-promulgated systems for arbitrating a broad range of employment-based disputes and issues. Employers rapidly developed dispute settlement arbitration systems to steer their employees away from the enforcement agencies and the courts and into arbitration. Some were laudable efforts to provide fair and rapid resolution of disputes that might otherwise languish in a clogged agency and judicial system, with resultant delays and heavy costs on all participants. Other plans constituted inequitable and oppressive efforts to tilt the result of such arbitrations to the employer, while depriving employees of many rights usually associated with due process and fairness. Chapter Five contains an examination of such systems and considers whether such mandatory procedures can be adjudged as fair if they must be agreed to as a condition of gaining or maintaining employment—that is, well before the employee has any knowledge of a potential statutory violation.

It was out of the mounting evidence of the lack of access to fairness and statutory protection that the Commission on the Future of Worker-Management Relations proposed the establishment of systems of statutory dispute resolution with due process protection. And it was from those recommendations that the Due Process Task Force met from September 1994 to May 1995 to develop the *Due Process Protocol of Mediation and Arbitration of Statutory Disputes Arising out of the Employment Relationship*, referred to elsewhere in this volume as the *Protocol*, establishing standards of fairness to be adopted for resolving employment based statutory disputes. The task force included representatives of the American Arbitration Association (AAA), the American Bar Association (ABA), the American Civil Liberties Union (ACLU), the Federal Mediation and Conciliation Service (FMCS), the National Academy of Arbitrators (NAA), the National Employment Lawyers Association, and the Society for Professionals in Dispute Resolution.

Chapter Six explains the evolution of the *Protocol*, its essential components, and the impact it has had on the employment scene, having been accepted by participating organizations, government agencies, and the neutral designating agencies as the minimal standards under which employment disputes will be resolved. (Appendix B gives the full text of the document.) Both the AAA and the other major organization that provides arbitrators, Judicial Arbitration and Mediation Service/Endispute (J.A.M.S./Endispute), have embraced the *Protocol* as the basic standard for administering mediation and arbitration of statutory disputes. Indeed, they have both gone beyond that narrow application to employ the *Protocol* for their administration of the full range of employment disputes, even those beyond statutory issues.

It should be emphasized that in any procedure for dispute resolution, mediation is a central element. The grievance procedure under collective bargaining provides a process for finding the facts and focusing efforts to resolve a dispute by agreement. Mediation is a prerequisite to arbitration under the *Protocol* and in the new rules of J.A.M.S./Endispute and the AAA. It is also regarded as an essential component by the government agencies that have adopted the *Protocol* for their own dispute resolution procedures.

Although this volume devotes more attention to arbitration procedures because of arbitration's use as a substitute for administrative appeals and litigation of employment disputes, one should not underestimate the vitality of mediation as a superior procedure for reaching mutually acceptable resolution of employment disputes. Mediation and its use are well understood and more familiar for the broad range of employment and other disputes. Its application to the statutory dispute area is crucial to an effective structure for conflict resolution, and other volumes adequately describe its use, techniques, and application. The limited references to mediation in this volume are not intended to minimize its benefits for the parties—they merely underscore the emphasis on the more innovative procedures of due process arbitration when combined with mediation.

Despite the growth of employer-promulgated systems of alternative dispute resolution (ADR) over the past half-decade and the manner in which the majority of courts have endorsed such procedures, the administrative agencies concerned with employment law have been slow to recognize or to facilitate the expanding reliance on such procedures. Chapter Seven reports and seeks to understand some of the problems faced in efforts to secure agency adoption or endorsement of private dispute settlement systems with due process protections. Agencies have failed to respond adequately to the pressure of reduced budgets for statutory enforcement, increased case backlogs, and the growing costs of judicial appeal for ordinary workers. These pressures dictate that government agency officials review their attitudes and undertake to encourage mediation and arbitration of specified categories of statutory issues as the most effective means of extending full statutory protection to the tens of millions who otherwise have no realistic access to due process protection of their statutory rights.

The importance of such official reexamination of traditional hostility to private resolution of employment disputes is underscored by the success of those few agencies that have embraced mediation and arbitration as the preferred means of resolving disputes. These agencies have cut their backlogs, reduced their personnel and enforcement costs, and brought speedier and more equitable statutory enforcement to a broader spectrum of the workforce than could otherwise have gained access to such protections.

Chapter Eight describes the landmark commitment of the Massachusetts Commission Against Discrimination to apply the full range of *Protocol* protections in administering its statutory responsibility. This effort shows that it can be done. The Commission fully subscribed to the *Protocol*, including the provisions for selection and training of specialized panels of mediators and arbitrators. The rapid processing and resolution of cases in the first months of the commission's operation of this policy—and the overwhelming resolution of those disputes in the mediation step—should point the way for other agencies committed to bringing workplace justice to those who could not otherwise afford the time or expense. Appendix C provides a copy of the commission's formal policy statement on ADR.

The Department of Labor has experimented thus far with ADR and negotiated rulemaking to a limited extent. In 1992 the Department of Labor used in-house mediators to resolve OSHA and wage-hour violations in the Philadelphia Region. Despite the appraisal of success, however, the program was discontinued at that time. Following the commission's *Report and Recommendations* of December 1994, the Department of Labor in February 1997 announced for comment pilot programs to use mediation and arbitration in certain whistleblowing, Family and Medical Leave Act, and other cases. The EEOC entered into an agreement with the FMCS in 1995 to provide mediation in certain cases and to train EEOC staff in district offices in mediation skills. These forms of ADR were fully authorized by the Administrative Dispute Resolution statutes of 1990 and 1996 for certain categories of cases.

The final chapter, Chapter Nine, shows how these and other experiences can be expanded by educating the administrative agencies and the judiciary—and all those entrusted with implementing the rights provided by protective employment statutes—

to the potentials of mediation and due process systems of arbitration. We envisage an experimental period, building on the experience of recent years, to consider the wider application of such private adjudication to certain classes of employment disputes.

Certainly the existing employer-promulgated mediation and arbitration structures can be improved. They may gain even wider acceptance through voluntary implementation of the *Protocol*. Even those that conform to the standards set forth in the *Gilmer* decision can be reexamined to determine if they provide the requisite minimal standards of due process we would all want for ourselves. Even if employers do not make such improvements, the designating agencies, legislatures, and courts should assure that due process is provided in such systems. Other organizations that speak for the views of employees—women's groups, civil rights organizations, unions—may find a new and more effective procedure for representation of workers under such structures. A new class of arbitrators and mediators trained not only in dispute resolution but also in the provisions and regulations of each employment statute will need to emerge to provide more rapid resolution of a wider range of workplace disputes than dealt with in conventional union-management mediation and arbitration.

To help the reader keep track of the discussion, Appendix A provides a convenient list of the acronyms used repeatedly in the text. In addition, the text also spells out each of these acronyms the first time it appears.

While our purpose is to bring statutory protections to the millions who currently are denied their rights as a practical matter under employment statutes, the prospect of invoking the *Protocol* for employment dispute resolution has a potential far beyond the employment field. Mediation and arbitration implemented in conformity with the *Protocol* could be used for resolving statutory and regulatory disputes in the fields of health care, the environment, family protection, and other areas of societal concern. This volume simply sketches the directions and encourages the mutual accommodations that are required to achieve a new system starting from some promising recent beginnings. Resolution of workplace disputes is only the first step in bringing more justice to more people through a fair, affordable and expeditious procedure for conflict resolution.

History and Acknowledgments

Arnold Zack and John Dunlop have known each other for many years in the Harvard community and through the national organizations of labor representatives, managements, and neutrals. The thought processes leading to this book began in 1993, when the Clinton administration established the Commission on the Future of Worker-Management Relations with Dunlop as chair. The third question in the commission's mission statement asked "What, if anything, should be done to increase the extent to which workplace problems are directly resolved by the parties themselves, rather than through recourse to state and federal courts and government regulatory bodies?" The commission's May 1994 *Fact Finding Report* presented extensive data on employment regulation and litigation and various private and public alternatives for dispute resolution, posing a series of questions for further consideration.

Zack discussed this section of the *Fact Finding Report* with Dunlop, and as president of the NAA he set about seeking to get a consensus on an appropriate system of employment law dispute resolution, building on private mediation and arbitration, that would overcome many of the shortcomings of many employer-promulgated plans. He presented his views to the Commission in hearings on September 29, 1994, before the *Report and Recommendations* were made public in January 1995.

During the first week of August 1994, Arnold Zack was urged by Helen Witt, Robert Segal, and Robert Manning—all old friends and participants in the Council of the Labor and Employment Law Section—to pay a courtesy call at the ABA Annual Meeting in New Orleans. That was, apparently, the first visit by a sitting president of the NAA to the ABA. His hosts at that conference, Chris

Barreca (a management lawyer now chair of the section) and Max Zimny (general counsel of the Union of Needletrades, Industrial and Textile Employees), endorsed the idea of private mediation and arbitration to resolve employment law disputes, and proposed a task force of representatives from like-minded organizations dedicated to the establishment and preservation of due process standards in employment arbitration. Invitations were issued and in September 1994 the new task force met at the New York offices of the AAA.

The task force continued to meet throughout the winter of 1994–1995, shifting from a clearinghouse to an action group as it came to realize that the representatives shared similar views of due process, felt such standards could be codified, and believed they should proclaim such unanimity to those charged with the responsibility of developing dispute settlement procedures in the employment field. The task force was unable to agree on the triggering event for the introduction of such protections, that is, whether the agreement to arbitrate should be pre- or postdispute, but it did agree on the due process protections to be provided once the arbitration process was initiated. The group developed the *Protocol* described earlier, which was signed on May 9, 1995.

Since then Zack has sought to circulate word about the *Protocol* among potential users and leaders in the employment field. The Labor and Employment Law Section of the ABA, first under the Chairmanship of Leo Geffner, and then Charles (Butch) A. Powell III, and then Donald MacDonald, has had the *Protocol* on its agenda in dozens of meetings of its committees and council. The NAA and the Industrial Relations Research Association have also highlighted the effort. Thomas Kochan of MIT, who was president of the International Industrial Relations Association, made it a focus of his presidential address and of the Washington D.C. meetings in 1995.

Our efforts to expand interest in the *Protocol* since the summer of 1995 have had both a state and a federal focus. The Massachusetts Commission Against Discrimination served as the state model for introducing due process mediation and arbitration. No one could have been more receptive, more perceptive, and more effective than Chairman Michael Duffy, who announced the program on February 14, 1996—within ten weeks of our initial discussion. The Secretary of Labor's Task Force on Excellence in State and Local Government Through Labor-Management Cooperation, in its June 1996 report, recommended and elaborated on the standards of the *Protocol* for employment law administered by state and local governments. The federal focus following the commission's *Report and Recommendations* was directed toward the development of a few pilot programs in the Department of Labor to employ voluntary mediation and arbitration in the adjudication of employment law disputes. Discussions were held with the task force and Chairman of the EEOC as the agency has considered the use of voluntary mediation and other ADR methods to resolve its large volume of cases.

Another focus to our efforts sought changes within the private agencies that typically designate arbitrators or furnish lists of arbitrators, namely the AAA and J.A.M.S./Endispute. J.A.M.S./Endispute adopted the *Protocol* standards and announced it would only administer arbitrations consistent with the *Protocol*. In May 1996, under the leadership of George Friedman, who had been an original Task Force member, the AAA also announced that it would administer cases only under a new set of employment rules that replicated *Protocol* standards. While the new rules of both organizations do provide due process protections for claimants in discrimination cases, they go much further. For the first time employees who signed arbitration agreements at the commencement of their employment are assured that *Protocol* rules will govern their claims regardless of any lesser standard they may have signed at the time of employment. Employers with arbitration plans with lesser standards have been able to invoke the name of the AAA or J.A.M.S./Endispute to give credibility to their own structures, knowing the agencies would administer their prescribed arbitration agreement rules. Such employers must now either abide by the due process standards of the AAA or J.A.M.S./Endispute rules or seek other administrators. Employee claimants under such programs have secured due process protections not only in discrimination cases, but in the much broader range of cases covered by employer-promulgated systems.

Arnold Zack is pleased to acknowledge the help and assistance offered by dedicated friends along the way. George Friedman, Christine Newhall, and Rick Reilly of the AAA, and Cliff Palefsky of the National Employment Lawyers Association, remain steadfast in their belief that the *Protocol* is the proper course for the future, despite transitory impediments. He also appreciates the financial assistance provided by the Hewlett Foundation through the Sloan School of Management at MIT and the Jacob Wertheim Fellowship in Industrial Relations at Harvard University to facilitate the research and writing of this book.

We acknowledge the vital assistance of Marie Stroud of Harvard, who was, of course, the vital and ever upbeat communication link between the authors at the computer and by voice, fax, and e-mail. She, in turn would like to thank Michele duBois and Ann Flack of the Harvard Economics Department for their technical expertise and support.

June 1997   JOHN T. DUNLOP
                                                Belmont, Massachusetts

                                                ARNOLD M. ZACK
                                                Boston, Massachusetts

The Authors

John T. Dunlop is Lamont University Professor, Emeritus, Harvard University, where he was chairman of the Department of Economics, 1961–1966, and dean of the Faculty of Arts and Sciences, 1970–1973.

He was director of the Cost of Living Council (Wage and Price Controls), 1973–1974; Secretary of Labor, 1975–1976; and chairman of the Pay Advisory Committee, 1979–1980, and of the Commission on the Future of Worker-Management Relations, 1993–1995.

He was president of the Industrial Relations Research Association, 1960–1961, and of the International Industrial Relations Association, 1973–1976.

He has been appointed as member or chairman of numerous government boards on industrial relations disputes.

He is the author of *Industrial Relations Systems* (1993 rev. ed.), coauthor of *Industrialism and Industrial Man* (1960), and author of *Dispute Resolution, Negotiation and Consensus Building* (1984), and other volumes.

Arnold M. Zack is a full-time arbitrator and mediator of labor-management disputes and is a past president of the National Academy of Arbitrators. He holds degrees from Tufts College, Yale Law School, and Harvard's J. F. Kennedy School of Government, and currently teaches alternative dispute resolution at Yale Law School and the Harvard Trade Union Program. Since 1993, he has served as the chairman of Bermuda's Essential Industries Dispute Settlement Board and has helped to develop dispute settlement machinery in a number of countries including Australia, Greece, South Africa, and Spain. He was a Fulbright Professor at Haile Selassie University in Ethiopia and has published ten books on labor training in developing countries as well as on labor-management mediation and arbitration. He was the initiator of the *Protocol* and has been active in encouraging its adoption here and abroad. Among his awards are the Cushing-Gavin Award of the Archdiocese of Boston, the Distinguished Service Award of the American Arbitration Association, and the Mildred Spaulding Award for three successive years for outstanding preserves of fruits and vegetables.

Mediation and Arbitration
of Employment Disputes

Chapter One

The Rise of Labor-Management Dispute Resolution

Mediation and arbitration, now standard to resolve private disputes between management and employees represented by unions, developed gradually over the past century. If these approaches are to be extended to resolve disputes over the application of employment statutes and regulations as we advocate here (with some exceptions), it is vital to identify the elements that created their present success.

Workers and their unions as well as management and their supervisory personnel had to learn by hard experience that they could minimize their own costs in time, money, and stress if they followed a prescribed grievance procedure, first developing facts and seeking a common settlement and then resorting to arbitration if the initial efforts failed to reach a solution. All the alternatives— overt strikes or lockouts, slowdowns or other disruptive tactics, or court action to resolve disputes—were more trouble and generally produced less satisfactory results for each side. Also, both workers and management learned to distinguish between disputes over the application of a collective agreement and disputes over the terms of the contract itself. They came to learn likewise that the commitment to arbitrate grievances would generally encourage direct mediation and settlement by their representatives. Further, a cadre of experienced neutrals began to emerge, acceptable to and respected by the parties. In time, the major administrative agency concerned with relations between unions and management, the National Labor Relations Board (NLRB),* decided to defer to

---

*A list of acronyms used in this book appears in Appendix A.

arbitration under an existing collective agreement where an unfair labor practice charge presented a similar issue.[1] Finally, the Supreme Court recognized that disputes as to the meaning and application of the agreement were best left, when within the "four corners of the agreement"—that is, within the intent of the agreement—to final resolution by arbitration.

Thus mediation and arbitration under collective agreements grew out of the mutual interest of the participants. It was to everyone's advantage to resolve disputes that arose between managements and unions in a timely fashion and by private means. This decentralized and private system was neither designed by legislators nor imported from other countries, either of which would probably have produced some form of labor court; rather, it was made by U.S. labor and management.

As Archibald Cox observed in 1960, "One reflecting upon the role of law in the administration of collective bargaining agreements can hardly avoid beginning with the thought that the institutions of collective bargaining evolved and flourished outside the courts and often in the face of legal interference."[2] It was only after the institutions of grievance procedures and arbitration were well established by labor and management in the interpretation and application of collective bargaining agreements, after a presidential conference of labor and management representatives in 1945 had endorsed such procedures, and after almost all collective agreements contained these provisions that the legal system through the Supreme Court in 1960 provided status and deference to arbitration awards and to arbitrators.[3]

This chapter is divided into four sections. The first traces the origins and meaning of mediation and arbitration and other terms used in dispute resolution of labor-management disputes. The second gives a brief sketch of the development of mediation and arbitration in the private sector prior to 1940, while the third assesses the impact of the National War Labor Board in the World War II period and the fourth analyzes the extension of mediation and arbitration of labor-management disputes to the public sector.

Forms of Dispute Resolution

Since the terminology of dispute resolution and related processes have substantially changed in meaning over the years, it is essential to identify these developments and the current usages. Arbitration is of ancient origins—the contending parties agree voluntarily to submit a dispute to a neutral party for decision and agree to comply with the decision. Forms of arbitration arose in early trading civilizations and found their way from the nomenclature of the Roman period of commerce to England. This strand of development led to maritime and commercial arbitration.[4] But it is dispute resolution in the setting of the workplace that is the present interest.

Arbitration

The early usage of *arbitration* in the workplace included what is now called *collective bargaining*, a term first used by Sidney and Beatrice Webb in England in 1891 but not found in general use in the United States until after the turn of the century. "Arbitration" was applied "to all settlements of labor disputes by conference committees of the parties as well as through decisions of the outsiders."[5] As the Webbs cautioned, "The student should note that there has been, until quite recently, no clear distinction drawn between Collective Bargaining, Conciliation and Arbitration. Much of what is called Arbitration or Conciliation in the earlier writings on the subject amount to nothing more than organized Collective Bargaining."[6]

Some labor leaders of the late nineteenth century in this country were in favor of "compulsory arbitration" in the sense of requiring employers to deal with the union or to have a compulsory investigation of a dispute by an impartial body; both parties were to remain free, however, to decide whether or not to accept a settlement.[7] In the current setting, compulsory arbitration has a very different meaning: the requirement by law to submit a dispute to a neutral arbitrator and to abide by the decision.

At an early date some practitioners of collective bargaining (but not all) came to distinguish between arbitration in the sense of adjudicating the terms and conditions to be incorporated in an agreement (now called *interest arbitration*) and arbitration as the resolution of disputes over the meaning and application of a collective bargaining agreement (now usually termed *grievance arbitration* or *rights arbitration*).

John Mitchell, president of the United Mine Workers, used arbitration in the current sense of grievance arbitration in this statement, from 1903:

> Joint agreements are, in fact, treaties of peace determining the conditions under which the industry will be carried on for a year, although longer agreements have been made and maintained. The agreement usually provides for the settlement or arbitration of all controversies which may arise under it. It is provided, however, that the arbitration shall be in the nature, not of negotiation, not of a change in the conditions fixed by the agreement, but shall be limited entirely to the interpretation of the agreement. . . . During the course of the dispute, however, the men remain at work, and as a result of the trade agreement and of the provisions therein contained for the adjustment of all questions in controversy, the number of petty local strikes has been minimized and conflicts of this nature have almost entirely disappeared.[8]

But this sharp distinction between what might be called the legislative function of negotiating collective agreements and the judicial function of interpretation is simplistic in a variety of circumstances. Collective agreements may be silent on many issues of "wages, hours, and conditions of employment." Past practices and procedure may be clearly or ambiguously identified. Parties may define and limit narrowly the scope of the authority of the arbitration body (as confined strictly to the interpretation of the language of the agreement) or much more broadly (as empowered to resolve any dispute arising during the period of the agreement). The provisions of collective agreements may broadly or narrowly define matters of management rights, union rights, or matters of joint determination. Arbitration bodies may include one or more neutrals or they may include representatives of the parties who negotiated the agreement. In some circumstances, impartial umpires have been involved in both the interpretation of current agreements and in the resolution of disputes over new agreements. These distinctions may be further complicated by the rulings of the NLRB and the courts over the statutory obligation to bargain collectively.[9]

Moreover, grievance arbitration does not necessarily preclude all strikes or lockouts during the term of a collective bargaining agreement. Indeed, some agreements carefully prescribe that certain issues—such as workloads, the speed of assembly lines, health and safety conditions, or even a final step in a grievance procedure—may be resolved by resort to strike or lockout.[10]

The preceding discussion depicts grievance and interest arbitration as arising from a voluntary collective bargaining process between labor and management with potential resort to the strike and lockout. However, some mediation and arbitration procedures historically arose from the pressure of government executives and legislatures concerned with the adverse consequences on the public welfare of specific conflicts and stoppages of work.

Government Design of Dispute Resolution

In what has been called "the most famous of all arbitration cases in this country," President Theodore Roosevelt intervened after a five-month coal strike in 1902. He called on the miners and operators to "meet upon the common plane of the necessities of the public." He proposed arbitration, and appointed the Anthracite Coal Strike Commission. The award settled the (interest) dispute and also provided for the establishment of grievance machinery and a permanent bipartisan Anthracite Conciliation Board—with a neutral umpire in case of a deadlock—which was "the first permanent machinery ever established in this country for the interpretation and application" of an agreement.[11]

Governmental pressures and requirements for the settlement of labor-management disputes over the provisions of collective agreements have taken a variety of forms. There have been seventy-one instances of federal government seizure of business properties in such disputes since the Civil War.[12] In 1916 the Congress enacted the Adamson Act, under threat of a national strike by the railroad brotherhoods, establishing the basic eight-hour day.[13] After the investigation and recommendations of a presidential commission and various emergency boards, the long-standing controversy over the manning of firemen on railroad diesel engines was resolved by legislation requiring that the dispute be settled by arbitration. Congress has on a number of occasions voted to order arbitration or to determine substantively the terms of employment in disputes in the railroad industry that have exhausted the procedures of the Railway Labor Act without resolution.[14]

The government interest in resolving labor-management disputes has taken other forms in the activity by state governments and the federal government in promoting machinery to resolve disputes by mediation and voluntary arbitration short of mandatory prohibition of the strike or lockout. By 1938, such laws were to be found in thirty-five of the forty-eight states, although in 1932 Witte wrote: "all told, the work of the state adjustment agencies must be put down as negligible."[15] In 1886, Massachusetts (with New York) was the first to establish a full-time Board of Conciliation and Arbitration. The Massachusetts board was generally regarded as the most effective; it was active in 419 cases between 1888 and 1904. In addition to voluntary conciliation and arbitration, this board provided technical arbitration in the settlement of piece rate questions in a number of local industries, most notably the shoe and leather industries.[16]

In 1913, the U.S. Conciliation Service was established as a part of the new Department of Labor. It was basically an agency for mediation; it also developed staff arbitration[17] until barred from that activity by statute in 1947, and it established procedures to provide lists of arbitrators on joint requests of labor and management. The 1947 Taft-Hartley Act (in Title II) made the Concilia-

tion Service an independent agency—the FMCS—outside the
Labor Department.

Conciliation

Conciliation is a term seldom used today and then usually—but not
always—interchangeably with *mediation*. At one time mediation
was regarded as a passive act of intervention between disputants by
a third party whereas conciliation was the attempt to reconcile the
disputants and bring about an agreement. "Mediation is a go-
between performing messenger service" while "conciliation makes
suggestions and offers advice on the controversial issues."[18] The
Massachusetts Board of Conciliation and Arbitration historically
used conciliation in this sense of actively urging parties to settle.
The ambiguity in the term conciliation is further illustrated by the
current Ohio statute, which provides in the case of public safety
services for the appointment of a conciliator whose settlement
award is a binding mandate on the parties.[19] *Mediation* currently is
the common term used to describe efforts of a neutral to secure voluntary settlement short of the authority to impose a settlement.

Development of Mediation and
Arbitration Prior to 1940

This section briefly describes the wide variety of types and characteristics of dispute resolution machinery that emerged in the relations of labor and management in the first part of this century,
reflecting diverse problems and opportunities of these sectors at the
time. There was no single pattern of evolution; rather a variety of
arrangements emerged to flourish and at times to recede. Of particular interest for the private sector are the development of the
impartial umpire, legislated railroad adjustment boards, systems of
interest arbitration, and ad-hoc interest arbitration.

The Umpire and Associates

The 1903 bipartite Anthracite Coal Board, with its neutral umpire,
was set up so that the labor and management members tried to
reach agreement on their own, resorting to the umpire only in case

of a deadlock. The labor and management members did settle most matters brought to the board, but they failed in twenty-five cases in the first nine years. The U.S. Commissioner of Labor was the umpire in all but one of these cases.[20] The umpire had a remote and impersonal relation to the parties, with disputes being submitted in writing for a ruling. Disputes over the terms of the collective agreement were beyond the scope of the board and the umpire.

"It was the apparel industries—clothing, millinery, hosiery, etc. which proved to be the great testing laboratory for private labor arbitration."[21] The Protocol of Peace of 1910 ended a major strike in the New York cloak and suit industry and provided for continuing arbitration machinery that considered grievances and at times disputes over contract terms and even disputes among the various associations of employers. The New York clothing agreements contained no explicit expiration date. The machinery operated at two levels, a bipartite body to resolve many grievances including piecerate disputes, and a board of arbitration with a neutral chairman. The New York clothing arbitration machinery was in frequent difficulty at the outset.[22]

The Hart, Schaffner, and Marx agreement likewise ended a Chicago marketwide strike in 1911. The arbitration machinery set up under the agreement, with the assistance of a bipartite trade board to handle piece rates and ordinary grievances, was an outstanding success from the outset. The collective agreements were of limited time duration and the arbitration board initially had no responsibility for the terms of the agreement, although it did at a later period. These clothing industries all involved their umpires directly and personally in dispute resolution, including informal mediation.

Arbitration came late in 1929 to the full-fashion hosiery industry. George W. Taylor served as impartial chairman for the period 1931–1941.[23] In the tradition of the clothing industries, the parties sought a chairman to act in the role of conciliator, mediator, friend, counselor—and only as a last resort as arbitrator. The arbitration machinery had no responsibility for the terms of the agreement, but the umpire did on occasion offer mediation suggestions during negotiations.

In these instances of bipartite boards with neutral and continuing umpires in clothing industries, the parties together selected and compensated the umpire. In the anthracite coal case, in contrast, the arbiter was to be selected by one of the judges of the Third Judicial Circuit.

The impartial umpireship was generally developed under multiemployer agreements (anthracite coal, men's and women's clothing, hosiery, shoes) where both parties on occasion had difficulty in controlling their members. The machinery was designed in part to provide uniform application of the agreement among competing firms. To jump ahead of the story a bit, in the post–World War II era the umpireship came to be adapted to large industrial enterprises with multiplant agreements with a single union.

In the case of umpires working with representatives of each party, the distinction between arbitration of grievances and arbitration of issues of interest was not always drawn sharply as at present. In part this arose out of the role of the umpire as a mediator and consultant to each side. But it also derived from the fact that collective bargaining agreements, as in England historically and in the U.S. railroad industry, were in these industries sometimes written without a specified expiration date. The agreement continued until one party served notice of a desire to change its terms.

Legislated Railroad Adjustment Boards

During the government operation of the railroads in World War I, 1917–1920, the Railway Administration made a clean-cut distinction between controversies over changes in wages, hours, and working conditions and those arising from the interpretation and application of agreements and grievances. To decide the latter disputes, three bipartisan boards of adjustment were established according to occupations, with appeal to the director-general in case of deadlock.[24]

The Transportation Act of 1920 permitted the continuation of adjustment boards by agreement, and the Act of 1926 made their establishment mandatory. But the railroad unions insisted on national boards, and the carriers favored boards by carrier system and region. Moreover, being bipartite, the boards that were created often found themselves in a deadlock with no way to resolve the dispute.

The Railway Labor Act amendments of 1934 provided for a National Railroad Adjustment Board divided into occupational divisions, and for the appointment by the National Mediation Board of impartial chairmen to serve as referees—not as continuing umpires. As in other industries, the railroad unions gave up the right to strike over so-called minor disputes in exchange for mandatory arbitration. Unlike any other private industry, even the airlines under the same statute, the parties in the railroad industry pay nothing for these Adjustment Board arbitrations; the government bears the expenses.[25]

Systems of Interest Arbitration of Collective Agreements

National unions and national employer associations emerged in a number of industries with local collective bargaining. These national groups in a number of sectors elected to establish machinery to resolve disputes over the provisions of local collective agreements. The daily newspaper field was notable for the American Newspaper Publishers Association and the Printers (International Typographical) Union. In 1901, the two entered into a national arbitration agreement that was renewed for twenty years. The initial agreement was limited to disputes over the meaning and application of local agreements. Subsequent national agreements were extended to cover the negotiation of local collective bargaining agreements. Impartial chairmen were often chosen from the local community in which the dispute arose.[26]

Another arrangement is illustrated by the national machinery between the National Electrical Contractors Association and the International Brotherhood of Electrical Workers. By 1921, these organizations had established a bipartite national council of representatives of both sides to resolve disputes over the provisions of local collective bargaining agreements as well as questions of interpretation and application of these agreements. In a strict sense, this machinery could be designated as pure conciliation—no arbitrator or continuing umpire is involved and all disputes that cannot be settled by the local parties have been directly resolved at the national level.

The street railway industry, which operates without an overarching national agreement, illustrates a still different arrangement for interest arbitration. The constitution of the national union became the mechanism for the implementation of a national policy favoring arbitration of the terms of collective agreements. The national union would not authorize a work stoppage if the management had offered arbitration. The development was influenced by the fact that many street railway operations were publicly owned and operated, and the industry was sensitive to public concerns with work stoppages.

A streetcar strike was avoided in Detroit in 1891 by an ad hoc agreement to arbitrate. W. D. Mahon, leader of the Detroit local—later the long-time president of the Amalgamated Association of Street Railway Employees—was a strong advocate of arbitration. The vast majority of collective agreements in the industry came to include a provision requiring arbitration before a tripartite arbitration board, locally established, in the event that direct negotiations over a new agreement failed to reach a settlement. These provisions in local collective bargaining agreements came to be an ongoing commitment to dispute resolution without a work stoppage.

Ad Hoc Interest Arbitration

Aside from such national systems, interest arbitration developed case by case. Resort to interest arbitration was accepted in particular circumstances as a result of the influence of government or private mediators, pressure of public opinion, or joint labor-management preference for avoiding confrontation. Particularly in the first decade of this century, the National Civic Federation, which included business, labor, and public leaders, maintained a Division of Mediation and Conciliation that promoted local boards of conciliation seeking to avert or settle strikes by conciliation and arbitration. The conciliation work of the Civic Federation in 1905 and 1906 extended to twenty-two states.[27]

In the building industry, the Bricklayers (union) and the Master Masons (employers) established Joint Committees of Arbitration as early as the 1880s and 1890s in the cities of New York, Chicago, and Boston to settle disputes over the terms of employment and to resolve other disputes. In most years these parties were able to settle these issues by direct negotiations. On occasion, as in Chicago in 1887—after a nine-week strike—they jointly selected an umpire (Judge Tuley of the Superior Court of Cook County) to resolve the dispute by unanimous agreement of all members of the committee. This particular Joint Committee of Arbitration also established a continuing Joint Standing Committee, with an umpire, to resolve all grievances.[28] Machinery of arbitration for the entire Chicago construction market was established by an agreement of 1915 that established the Joint Conference Board.[29] One of the most far-reaching arbitration awards with a neutral was made in 1921 by Judge Kenesaw Mountain Landis, later baseball commissioner, on wage rates and the controversial subject of various work rules.[30]

The growth of both interest and grievance arbitration in the period before 1940 contributed to the establishment of the AAA in 1926, although the expansion in commercial arbitration—referred to at the outset of this chapter—was the larger factor. In 1937, the AAA established its Voluntary Industrial Tribunal, which maintained a panel of labor-management arbitrators available to the parties.

The development of arbitration in the private sector in this early period followed no single or standard pattern. In some instances a sharp distinction was made between issues of interpretation and interest arbitration while other arrangements considered both. Some agreements had fixed durations while others continued until notice to reopen. Some agreements were multiemployer and others were confined to a single employer or workplace. In railroads, legislation designed the process. The impartial umpire, confined to interpretations of an agreement, probably bears closer resemblance to current grievance arbitration, although grievance arbitration was relatively rare in agreements in the prewar period. But precedents in the period exist for most features of contemporary labor-management mediation and arbitration.

The War Years, 1940–1953

The period 1940 to 1953 saw a succession of federal government dispute-settling agencies, including nonstatutory fact-finding boards and wage and salary stabilization authorities: the National Defense Mediation Board (March 19, 1941 to January 12, 1942), the National War Labor Board (January 12, 1942 to December 31, 1945), the National Wage Stabilization Board (January 1, 1946 to February 24, 1947), and the Wage Stabilization Board (September 9, 1950 to February 6, 1953). While the powers and policies of these agencies differed, they were all tripartite, comprising members drawn from labor unions, managements, and neutrals in labor-management disputes. This was also a period of rapid expansion in the membership of labor organizations and the spread of collective bargaining to mass production industries, with many new employees and new labor-management relationships. Union membership expanded from 7.1 million in 1940 to 16.4 million in 1953.[31]

On July 1, 1943, the War Labor Board issued a statement that declared in part that the Board,

As the custodian of the no-strike no-lockout agreement, and as a part of the all-out effort to win the war, calls upon the parties to all labor agreements to accept this urgent responsibility and render this patriotic service.

1. To install adequate procedures for the prompt, just, and final settlement of the day-to-day grievances involving the interpretation and application of the contract.

2. To make the full functioning of the grievance procedure a major responsibility under the no-strike no-lockout agreement for the maximum production to win the war.[32]

As a matter of policy, War Labor Board orders provided for an effective grievance procedure in all collective bargaining agreements. The orders also provided for the use of arbitration as the final step.[33]

The Labor-Management Conference called by President Truman in October 1945 was an indication of the enhanced support by labor and management organizations for grievance arbitration in the private sector. Although the conference disagreed on many matters, a unanimous report stated: "Collective-bargaining agreements should contain provisions that grievances and disputes involving the interpretation or application of the terms of the agreement are to be settled without resort to strike, lock-outs or other interruptions to normal operations by an effective grievance procedure with arbitration as the final step."[34]

A measure of the change in the status of grievance arbitration as a result of the policies of the wartime agencies and the attitudes of labor and management—the parties to collective bargaining agreements—is reflected in a comparison of the extent of arbitration as a final step in grievance procedures before World War II and after the Korean War. Sumner H. Slichter reported that "fewer than 8 to 10 percent of the agreements in effect in the early 1930s provided for arbitration as the final step of the grievance procedure."[35] By 1944, the U.S. Bureau of Labor Statistics found arbitration provisions in 73 percent of the agreements. This increased to 89 percent in 1952 and to 95 percent by 1960. It is today virtually universal, although the procedures, mechanisms, and scope vary substantially.

A further indication of the extent of grievance mediation and arbitration is reflected in the fact that in 1929 there were probably no more than a half-dozen permanent impartial umpires or chairmen in the whole country. In 1947 there were thirty-one permanent impartial chairmen in fifty-six industry groups in metropolitan New York alone.[36]

Mediation developed as a standard procedure to be applied before arbitration. The goal was to resolve significant numbers of grievances, particularly in labor-management relationships with a continuing arbitrator or impartial umpire.[37]

Notice also needs to be taken of the appointment by the federal government (on occasion by the president and often by the Secretary of Labor or the Director of the FMCS after 1947) of nonstatutory fact-finding boards to make recommendations for settlement of disputes over the terms of expired collective bargaining agreements, at times with work stoppages under way. These boards typically comprised three experienced neutrals. In the nine months after the end of hostilities in 1945, twelve boards were appointed. The 1947 Taft-Hartley Act, in Title II, provided for Boards of Inquiry in disputes held to imperil the nation's health or safety, but the Act precluded the boards from making any recommendation. The report of the facts was to be used to seek an injunction against a strike or lockout for sixty days.

Another significant development of the 1940–1953 period was the rapid growth of a cadre of professional arbitrators. Most of them were veterans of the wartime labor-management dispute-settling agencies. But a few were established neutrals before World War II—most notably George W. Taylor,[38] William M. Leiserson,[39] and Harry A. Millis[40]—and helped to shape the standards for the rising profession and the arbitration systems in the recently organized industrial workplaces. In 1947 a number of these new professionals established the National Academy of Arbitrators.[41]

Mediation and Arbitration in the Public Sector

Unlike the long evolution of private sector mediation and arbitration in various forms over the past century, arbitration of labor-management disputes in government employment is largely a product of the era beginning about 1960. Further, the dictum of the Supreme Court that "the agreement to arbitrate grievance disputes is the *quid pro quo* for an agreement not to strike"[42] scarcely can serve as the basis for arbitration involving government employees—who generally have had no right to strike. Then there was always the doctrine of sovereignty to fuel arguments that public officials cannot abdicate their authority to outside arbitrators. Further, civil service systems were seen as establishing procedures to determine all matters affecting the terms of public employment not specified by legislation.

It may appear in these circumstances somewhat surprising that in 1995 43.5 percent of the 18.4 million government employees were represented by labor organizations[43] and covered by collective bargaining agreements that generally included grievance procedures with arbitration,[44] although the range of subjects and the authority of the arbitration machinery, particularly in federal employment, is much narrower than in the private sector. In state and local governments that have statutes authorizing collective bargaining for some or all occupations of public employees, interest arbitration has also grown substantially within circumscribed limits in many jurisdictions.[45]

There were some early cases of city governments voluntarily agreeing to arbitration, as Pittsburgh did during World War I following a strike of firefighters over wages.[46] Also, the record reflects several cases of individual discharge over the rights of self-organization in the National Recovery Administration in 1934 and the Federal Power Commission in 1936. These cases led to advisory arbitration and a determination of anti-union discrimination in proceedings before federal government agencies involved in private labor-management dispute resolution, and to the reemployment of two individuals.[47]

But the War Labor Boards, in both World War I and II, regarded public employment disputes or government employee grievances as beyond their jurisdiction. As the War Labor Board stated in 1942: "The well established doctrines of American law pertaining to the sovereign rights of state and local governments clearly exclude such disputes from the jurisdiction and powers of the Board."[48] The war periods did not lead to the same vast expansion of grievance arbitration in governments as in the private sector.

Further, the Boston police strike of 1919 evoked long-lived public hostility to strikes by public employees. As Massachusetts Governor Calvin Coolidge said, "There is no right to strike against the public safety by anybody, anywhere at anytime." President Roosevelt's statement of 1937 is more general but no less explicit: "Since their own services have to do with the functioning of the government, a strike of public employees manifests nothing less than an attempt on their part to prevent or obstruct the operations of government until their demands are satisfied. Such actions looking toward the paralysis of government by those who have sworn to support it is unthinkable and intolerable."[49] In 1947 the Taft–Hartley Act banned strikes in the federal service and made such action a possible felony. President Reagan's action in the air controllers' strike of August 1981 reflected the same attitudes.

After World War II, labor organizations expanded among public employees in federal, state, and local governments. Postal clerks and letter carriers had long developed organizations that sought to better conditions and resolve disputes largely by influencing legislative and administrative processes. Teachers developed associations that sought to influence local governments and later came to behave like unions. Firefighters and police formed associations and unions that interacted with local governments over improved conditions of employment. In their regular interaction with public officials, these labor organizations sought redress for many grievances on behalf of their members, ordinarily without resort to strike but often with considerable ingenious pressures.

These developments were to contribute to a new era of public employment relations in the 1960s. In 1962, President Kennedy issued Executive Order 10988 covering the federal service. It legitimized formal negotiating procedures, unit determination, exclusive recognition, written agreements, and procedures to determine unfair labor practices in the federal sector.[50] Wisconsin had pioneered in 1959 with a board like that described in the Labor-Management Relations Act (LMRA) for public employees. In the years 1965–1967, six more states—Connecticut, Delaware, Massachusetts,[51] Michigan, Minnesota, and New York[52]—adopted a modified LMRA model, including the obligation on the public employer to bargain and to participate in dispute resolution procedures. In most states, this stopped short of arbitration.

In 1967, the National Education Association, in moving to act more like a union, recognized strikes of affiliates as likely to occur and worthy of support. The International Association of Fire Fighters (IAFF) dropped the ban on strikes from its constitution in 1968.

The number of strikes in all governments went from 36 (with 28,600 workers) in 1960 to 412 (with 333,500 workers) in 1970—a number enlarged by the federal postal strike—and to 378 (with 180,700 workers) in 1976. Most of the stoppages were in local government.

The Bureau of Labor Statistics no longer publishes specialized government employee work stoppage data. But data for public employees in New York state reflect the sharp decline of these actions in the last fifteen years. The number of work stoppages averaged 20.9 per year in the decade 1971–1980; 3.6 per year in the decade 1981–1990, and 2.4 per year in the period 1991–1995. The average number of workers involved in these work stoppages each year in the three periods was 23,646, 733, and 323.[53] Work stoppages in governments do not appear to be a significant problem at this time.

When the 1970 Postal Reorganization Act created the U.S. Postal Service in place of the Post Office Department, it also restructured labor relations away from legislated terms and conditions of employment toward collective bargaining with a role for the NLRB for representation questions. Disputes over collective bargaining agreements were to be resolved by negotiations, mediation, and finally by arbitration. Arbitration awards over the terms of collective agreements in 1978, 1984, and 1990–1991 in the Postal Service included more workers than probably any other interest arbitration awards in this country.[54]

Clearly, after 1960 the attitudes of legislators, public officials, public employees, and their organizations were changing toward machinery for dispute resolution in the public sector. Strikes were still illegal and not recognized as a legitimate means to resolve disputes over wages and conditions of employment, but for a period many took place anyway and required a better means to resolve the underlying issues. Improvised case settlement procedures and high penalties were not an adequate policy. A more regularized procedure for recognition, negotiations, and dispute resolution came to be recognized as the preferred choice, particularly in industrial states with substantial union organization in the private sector.[55]

Dispute resolution started with mediation and fact-finding and tended to evolve—particularly for firefighters and police—into some forms of arbitration, though more limited in the scope of issues than in the private sector. For instance, the 1966 Massachusetts statute provided no finality for disputes over the terms of collective agreements, but as a consequence of unresolved disputes in 1973, final and binding arbitration over contract issues was enacted for firefighters and police. The provision providing for municipal funding of all awards was eliminated by a state referendum in 1980, Proposition 2½, but was restored in part through legislation in 1987 providing that arbitration awards bind municipal executives but not municipal legislative bodies on the financial terms of an award. As collective agreements came to be standard, a grievance procedure and grievance arbitration were generally adopted with some constraints on issues to be arbitrated.

Twenty-three states have passed comprehensive public sector labor relations laws extending collective bargaining to all public employees at the state and local levels, and an additional thirteen states have passed more limited statutes granting more limited collective bargaining rights. States may also have right-to-work statutes. The states often have different policies for classes of employees—state employees, municipal employees, teachers, and police and fire personnel; there also may be different policies and procedures on grievances and interest disputes. Fourteen jurisdictions appear to have no collective bargaining statute. As to interest disputes involving public employees, there may be a mandatory provision for mediation, and in addition for fact-finding and on occasion for some forms of arbitration for some classes of employees. Some state statutes only provide for arbitration if mutually agreed. In some states, the rejection of a fact-finding report may lead at the request of either party to the submission of the dispute to the legislature for resolution, or to a binding judicial determination. (Some states provide that arbitration awards are advisory only as to money items.) Most states prohibit strikes for all or designated categories of employees. The extent and forms of interest arbitration are very diverse across states for various categories of public employees.[56]

It is not necessary here to decide the extent to which the changes in public sector labor-management relations after 1960 were the result of new public policy initiatives, the result of the activities of public employees, or the changing attitudes of the general public toward public labor-management relations. But interest arbitration in the public sector is a limited-purpose tool for dispute resolution, as Clark Kerr stated in a 1984 postal award: "Arbitration of interests, as this arbitration is, sometimes may be necessary. It is never desirable. Arbitration of interests, if it becomes the practice rather than the occasional exception, can become lethal in the long run. It is far better for the parties and the American society that the parties themselves write their own contracts."[57]

Summary

This country had a long period of experimentation with mediation and arbitration in labor-management disputes in the private sector before the Supreme Court in the 1960 *Steelworkers Trilogy* sanctified arbitration and the role of arbitrators in grievance resolution. Arbitration in the public sector is a much more recent development, particularly since the 1960s, having to overcome concerns over sovereignty and the civil service system and a preoccupation with the acceptability of the strike. In general, the scope of arbitration in the public sector is more limited than in the private sector.

This long evolution established the difference, not always made in an earlier era, between interest arbitration and grievance or rights arbitration in private industry collective bargaining. In the period prior to 1940 arbitration was seen primarily as a means to resolve actual and potential work stoppages over the provisions of collective agreements or over the forms of recognition to be provided by one side to the other. Interest arbitration remains largely an ad hoc matter, and negotiations over most collective bargaining agreements are settled through mediation or direct agreement of the parties before or following resort to self-help. Arbitration of agreements remains infrequent, except in state and municipal collective bargaining, and particularly in the public safety services and in the Post Office.[58]

The past created a wide variety of arbitration forms, procedures, and machinery: single arbitrators, umpires, panels of neutrals, and tripartite boards; written opinions as precedents or not; the role of mediation or formal procedures within arbitration; specialized machinery for particular issues such as piece rates or incentives or work jurisdiction; the last-best-offer choice or conventional authority to decide an issue presented by the parties; the time limits; and the allocations of costs and charges between the parties; and so on. Even similar forms of grievance arbitration in the same industry may work in very different ways.[59] The commitment to arbitration of grievances or terms of agreements often tends to enhance the prospects for settlement through mediation.

The development of a socially accepted system of dispute resolution under collective bargaining agreements provides a foundation for the emergence of an alternative system of dispute resolution over employment law and regulations. This history should help inform workers and their various advisors and representatives, managements, government agencies, mediators and arbitrators, and the courts as they interact to experiment with designs for an alternative system over the years ahead. The history also suggests that instead of a rigidly uniform procedure, a variety of arrangements may be appropriate to provide due process and equity in different settings and for particular parties.

Chapter Two

Labor-Management Arbitration as the Framework for Employment Law Dispute Resolution

Despite the varied forms of union-management mediation and arbitration in use today, both parties are generally content and regard their arrangements to be in their mutual interest. Indeed the institution of union-management arbitration has proven of such value to the parties and to the larger society that it is being adapted and applied to new fields—sports, environmental protection, financial institutions, landlord-tenant relations, and even domestic disputes. This widespread use could hardly have been foreseen by those who struggled over the decades to give credibility to mediation and arbitration. Here we turn to another potential application of union-management mediation and arbitration techniques, assessing their application and adaptability to disputes over employment law and regulations.

Complaints arising under employment law and regulations are currently subject to investigation by various government agencies. Each has quite distinctive procedures for adjudication prescribed by statute, subject to appeal to the regular court system. By contrast, grievances under collective agreements at a workplace enter a well-established procedure that runs through several clear steps with specified time limits, ending up if necessary in final and binding arbitration.

Statutory employment law processes involve long delays and substantial costs, and our current political climate makes it likely that the budgets of government enforcement agencies will be reduced still further rather than increased to meet the increasing workload. Compounding the problem, employment law tends to rely on the premise that government officials are totally dispassionate or adequately represent those who have been wronged, so that claimants must either accept agency representation or pay for their own representatives out of their own pockets. This premise adds to agency workload but it often fails to command support in the workplace, so that employees with grievances tend to regard themselves as disadvantaged if they cannot afford to hire their own representatives. They tend to be much more satisfied with union-management processes under a grievance procedure and arbitration, where the union provides representation for the grievant. Overall, the performance and general acceptability of employment law processes contrasts sharply with that of most grievance procedures.

The status of employment law mediation and arbitration is uncertain and in a formative stage. It is far from achieving the judicial respect for union-management mediation and arbitration over disputes within the "four corners of the agreement," which is fully established in law.

This chapter is divided into three sections. It discusses the strengths of mediation and arbitration in their potential application to employment law disputes, then turns to the limitations of mediation and arbitration in their potential application to employment law disputes. It concludes with the issues of the acceptability of mediation and arbitration to resolve employment law disputes outside of a collective bargaining relationship.

Strengths

Consider the advantages of applying the union-management methods of mediation and arbitration to the adjudication of employment law and regulations:

• *Arbitration maintains tranquility between disputing parties for the term of the agreement.* The traditional trade-off, whereby employees continue to work in exchange for the employer's commitment to abide by the award, has freed the economy from the uncertainty and chaos of wildcat stoppages or shutdowns. It has also fulfilled the expectation of providing employees and employers with a speedy, inexpensive alternative to the disruption and delays of litigation. Certainly, if applied to the resolution of statutory disputes, mediation and arbitration would provide a foreseeable routinized alternative to the uncertain and more expensive progression of disputes through agencies, courts, and judicial appeals.

• *Union-management arbitration assures the parties of a final and binding resolution of their dispute.* That finality is expressed in the form of a written opinion and decision directed to the parties answering the question they submitted to the arbitrator for resolution. That finality would be a welcome alternative at the workplace to the disruption and unrest of prolonged litigation and to the tendency of aggrieved employees to seek redress as ex-employees rather than to pursue their rights as continuing employees. Final and binding resolution of statutory disputes militates against the potential of a wealthy or more determined party outspending the other through unending appeals; time is seldom entirely neutral between the parties.

• *Union-management arbitration flourishes because it provides fairness and due process under standards that are the result of the parties' negotiated procedures.* Two parties who recognize they have a shared stake in the process can generally succeed in developing an equitable procedure for resolving their disputes. These standards may be modified over time by the interpretations and awards of arbitrators as well as by the review of the parties. Fairness was, after all, the parties' agreed-upon goal in establishing such a structure. They sought to avoid the power imbalance that would inevitably sour their relationship and lead to distrust of any structure in which one side was the inherent beneficiary.

In the nonunion sector, where there is no comparable equality between the employer and the individual employee, there is need for fair procedures. That is particularly important in the statutory field, where the protections of due process are essential to secure agency and judicial endorsement of the arbitrator's award. Since it is unreasonable to expect the ordinary individual employee to negotiate as an equal with an employer, adoption of the due process standards from the collective bargaining environment would alleviate to some degree the imbalance between employer and individual employee. As in the collective bargaining arena, arbitrators would fine-tune the procedures to assure the protection and continuation of due process in subsequent cases between employers and employees.[1]

  • *In union-management arbitration, the parties have a shared role in the selection of the arbitrator in accordance with the procedures they have negotiated.* They have a shared commitment to the result imposed by the arbitrator. The award is thus in part of their own doing and not something imposed by a stranger selected or imposed by others. The arbitrator may be negotiated into the agreement as the sole decider of all disputes throughout the life of the agreement. Or the parties may agree on a panel of neutrals and select one of them in rotation or by lot for successive cases. Finally, if the parties are not able to agree on a mutually acceptable arbitrator for a pending case, they may use the facilities of a neutral agency such as the AAA or the FMCS to provide a list of neutrals from which the choice can be made by alternate striking (where the parties take turns removing a name from the list until only one name remains) or by agency designation.[2]

Arbitration under collective agreements has resulted in the development of a cadre of neutrals acceptable to both parties. Although there are some 3,500 arbitrators on the rosters of the AAA and the FMCS, only about 16.4 percent work as full-time arbitrators, hearing an average of 63.77 cases per year. Members of the National Academy of Arbitrators (about 17 percent of the arbitrator population) decided an average of 55.7 cases apiece in 1986.[3] Approximately half the arbitrators are lawyers, while part-time arbitrators work as teachers of law, economics, management, or education, and in a variety of other activities. Arbitrators have become the scriveners of a whole body of industrial jurisprudence, recognized and respected by the courts, and used by the parties to guide their future relations so that they can resolve disputes without resort to the arbitration forum. The recurrent selection of the same arbitrators not only demonstrates the parties' faith in the integrity of arbitrators who ruled against them in prior cases, it also demonstrates the faith of the parties in a system that permits them their own selection of decision makers.

The field of ADR for employment law disputes thus far does not have comparable experience in jointly selecting or developing a cadre of experienced neutral arbitrators. Indeed, judging from reports in the press about arbitration in the securities industry and among large law firms, selection of arbitrators has been made by the employer in putting together the arbitration plan. The choice of the claimant has been limited to selection from a panel of such employer-designated arbitrators. An ADR structure could be developed to produce greater confidence in the neutrality of the arbitrators, greater expertise among arbitrators handling cases, and greater acceptance of the process itself. The outlines of such a structure are clear: a neutral agency should place potential arbitrators on a panel, drawing on a pool of people with training and competence in the employment law matters in question, and parties to disputes should have knowledge of the arbitrators' prior experience and should either share in the selection process or mutually agree upon some designating procedure.

If arbitration can be institutionalized for employment law disputes, it should be possible to develop the same type of professionalism among the arbitrators, using their skills and understanding of the employment field to create a comparable industrial jurisprudence for future guidance of employers and employees. An additional benefit of arbitration would be the opportunity for the parties to select their own decision maker. Such an arrangement would be preferable to being subject to the vagaries of agency and judicial assignments to cases where the judge may not have much training and experience in the field. Arbitrators would at least have been subject to specialized training and jointly selected because of that expertise. And when the courts scrutinize the structure and due process protections of such an arbitration system, one would expect that the independence and integrity of the employment law arbitrators will lead to the same sort of substantive deferral as has occurred by the NLRB in the collective bargaining realm.[4]

- *In union-management arbitration the parties reinforce the neutrality of the arbitrator by a traditional equal sharing of the arbitrator's fees and expenses.* In a few situations the parties have contractually negotiated for the loser to pay the full arbitrator's bill, but equal sharing is by far the accepted and preferred norm.[5] This arrangement avoids the potential for bias to a single payer who may be the source of future work by making the arbitrator equally obligated to both parties. It also provides the arbitrator with a sense of independence in knowing that future selection does not depend on the party paying the fee. The equal sharing also instills more trust in the arbitrator should there be consideration of future use of that neutral. Although the conventional wisdom is that an arbitrator so responsible to two parties will tend to split the difference to retain joint acceptability, the reality is that although the parties both like to think they have a winning case, there are times when one side realizes the other may have a stronger case. People are unlikely to give future trust to an arbitrator who seems to have decided in their favor on a case they thought they would lose, just to maintain a win-loss balance between the parties.[6] Pleasant as it is to win, it sours the victory if it seems likely that the next case—which may well be even more important—may be the other side's turn at victory.

The cost sharing prevalent in union-management grievance arbitration is difficult to arrange in the nonunion sector, where claimants lack such built-in institutional support. One of the most troublesome aspects of adapting union-management arbitration to the employment law field is replicating the parity of funding support for the arbitrator. Obviously the employer has greater resources. Authorizing the arbitrator to award payment of the arbitrator's fee as part of the award may be a means of solving the problem when the claimant wins. It does not solve the problem when the claimant loses or the arbitrator declines to charge the full costs to the employer. It would be ideal if each side could equally share in the compensation of the arbitrator in the employment field. Unfortunately, economic reality calls for developing alternative measures in the ADR field that will protect the parties from an arbitrator tilting toward the primary funder and the source of repeat work.

• *Union-management arbitration is faster and less expensive than litigation.* In union-management arbitration the parties have helped to create a system that avoids many of the burdens, costs, and delays of the legal system. The extensive use of grievance step meetings prior to the arbitration hearing encourages the parties fully to disclose their evidence and positions in repeated efforts to resolve the dispute. Such procedures are an appealing substitute for the costly and often time-consuming processes of court-ordered discovery and depositions. Additionally, it is routine for procedural and even substantive arbitrability to be presented to the arbitrator for resolution at the outset of the hearing, saving time and money that in litigation could be stretched over protracted preliminary court proceedings. The last—and probably the most time- and cost-saving—attribute of arbitration is its finality. The parties do not face the series of appeals that too often characterize litigation. Due to court acceptance of the process of union-management arbitration, there has been little need to turn to litigation except in rare cases where the arbitrator has exceeded prescribed jurisdiction or where there is a need for court enforcement of an award against a reluctant loser. Arbitration is a one-stop forum, with an arbitrator selected by the parties for his or her experience in the subject matter and ability to conduct expeditious hearings. It is both cheaper and more effective in bringing rapid closure to the parties' dispute.

The speed and economy attributes are certainly desirable for dispute resolution in the statutory area. When one looks at the state of claims in the discrimination area it is clear that access to relief through the administrative agencies and through the courts is both time-consuming and expensive. Indeed the very standing of the claimant in a nonunion setting demonstrates that cost disparity. As noted earlier, a claimant in the collective bargaining arena can turn to the union, which serves as advocate without charge to the grievant through the grievance procedure and arbitration. A claimant in a nonunion setting—assuming he or she even becomes aware of a viable claim—must secure representation and pay for it from the initiation of the claim through to the end of litigation, including perhaps through multiple appeals. Development of an ADR system may reduce those costs for the employee, perhaps by having the employer provide partial reimbursement of legal fees, or by having an enforcement agency provide assistance, or by arranging assistance from some other source—perhaps even through a professional organization, a community organization, or a neighboring union. But aside from the cost of representation, which can be substantial, employment ADR can be far less expensive and time-consuming than resort to the courts.

• *Imminent arbitration provides a crucial setting for more effective and fruitful mediation.* The prospect of surrendering control over a case to an outside arbitrator often constitutes sufficient inducement to the parties to resolve the dispute themselves. That has been the case in interest disputes where mediation against the backdrop of an impending strike or lockout has increased prospects of settlement. It is also the case in rights arbitration, where grievance mediation is often invoked to resolve grievances ripe for immediate arbitration. Litigants do often reach settlements on the courthouse steps, but the structured use of mediation improves the chances of settlement to avoid arbitration of statutory issues. Without the backdrop of an imminent decision, mediation is far less likely to succeed. That is particularly true if the backdrop instead is a multiyear wait for litigation and the absence of pressure to change or compromise positions.

• *Grievance arbitration to resolve a wide range of employee disputes—including disciplinary matters—has been growing in usage and acceptability in public sector collective bargaining agreements.* These disputes had previously followed the arcane and often arduous route of appeals through administrative agencies for resolution, with subsequent access to court review and potential court appeals. Public sector employers and employees now have a single forum for final and binding resolution of such disputes without drawn-out administrative procedures and lengthy and costly appeals. Furthermore, they now have the right to select their arbitrator from panels of qualified neutrals rather than run the risk of appealable decisions by political officials. Those same benefits of expedited procedures are attainable in the proposed arbitration of statutory issues.

From the foregoing discussion it should be apparent that there have been substantial benefits to the parties that created the union-management arbitration system. Those benefits go beyond cost savings and more expeditious conflict resolution. They include as well the provision of a system of fairness developed under the aegis of the parties and providing them with recognition that the surrender of authority to the arbitrator is likely to result in an equitable disposition of the dispute while the parties' work relationship continues unimpeded.

Limitations

Assessment of the strengths of union-management arbitration is not enough to form a judgment about its applicability to statutory disputes. It is also necessary to consider some of its limitations:

- *Union-management arbitration is a system limited by law for resolving wrongs.* The parties and the arbitrator can make presentations only on matters negotiated into the contract by the parties. That mandate may extend to resolving questions of whether or not an employee was disciplined or discharged for just cause, or whether the employer has been discriminatory in its treatment of employees under the contract. In such cases, the arbitrator's range of authority is restricted to the four corners of the agreement. Even if the arbitrator were to hold that the employer acted improperly in discriminating against an employee, the award must draw its essence from the parties' agreement. Also, arbitrator findings of statutory violations do not bind the administrative agencies or the courts. Thus an arbitrator's decision that an employer has violated a discrimination statute, even if the parties' agreement did grant the arbitrator the authority to interpret the statute, does not appear under present court decisions to bind either the agency administering that statute or the courts. Union-management arbitration does not bring statutory finality. It only binds the parties to the arbitrator's contractual finding. In 1974, the Supreme Court held that despite an adverse arbitration decision, the losing party still had statutory enforcement rights under the law, and the Court would not embrace the arbitrator's findings of law as its own.[7] It would give deference to the fact-finding role of the arbitrator, but reserved to the appropriate administrative agency and the courts the authority to determine whether or not there had been a statutory violation.

That limitation on the arbitrator's authority is not present in employment arbitration outside the collective bargaining agreement. Indeed, outside of collective bargaining the arbitrator appears to have far greater authority. In its 1991 *Gilmer*[8] decision, the Court endorsed a private agreement to arbitrate all disputes arising under a securities industry employment contract. So it seems that the courts are, or have become, more willing to defer to arbitration of employment issues than they were two decades ago. The legal implications of the two disparate decisions will be discussed in Chapter Four. Suffice it to say at this point that non–collective-bargaining arbitration has the strong endorsement of the courts. The question of whether all endorsed structures meet the standards of due process is very much a matter of concern.

• *Union-management arbitration covers a small percentage of the workforce.* In 1995, unions under collective bargaining agreements represented 18.3 million of the nation's nonagricultural wage and salary workers, or 16.7 percent. Accordingly, even if union-management arbitration were accepted as final resolution of statutory issues by the courts, such determinations would affect only a small portion of the workforce, hardly a way to bring about widespread statutory compliance.

However, arbitration in the nonunion setting does offer the prospect of broader protection of worker statutory rights. Given the attitude of the courts toward arbitration in the *Gilmer* decision, one could foresee far wider protection of employee statutory rights through a structured arbitration than is currently available to employees in the organized sector. The prospects for effective arbitration of statutory rights appear more promising in the unorganized than in the organized sector. Given the Supreme Court's 1974 unwillingness to defer statutory issues to arbitrators of collective bargaining agreements, the range of application under *Gilmer* could well run to the full workforce, whether or not unionized.

• *Labor-management arbitrators lack statutory expertise.* While many arbitrators are lawyers and the rest are well acquainted with many aspects of labor law, their role neither calls for nor includes jurisdiction over discrimination and other employment statutes. Labor-management arbitrators tend not to be familiar in detail with statutes, regulations, administrative agency rulings, or current court decisions involving employment law, since they can safely confine their concern to an arbitration jurisdiction comfortably restricted by the parties' agreement.

Outside the collective bargaining arena a much broader attention is required. If the courts continue to defer to arbitration awards on discrimination and other employment law issues, it will be essential to examine whether arbitrators are deciding cases in compliance with the applicable law and current regulations. In *Gilmer* the court did not go into that issue. Hopefully, arbitration in the nonunion sector will spread beyond the current employer-promulgated security industry type of arbitration to a stage where the administering agencies knowingly and voluntarily defer cases to experienced and trained arbitrators. At that stage it will be essential that arbitrators be conversant with the current status of the law, the applicable regulations, and the pertinent court decisions.

- *Union-management arbitration seems to be under increasing scrutiny by the courts.* Until recently, the courts refrained from looking over the arbitrator's shoulders to the merits of the pending dispute. The NLRB has adhered to a policy of deferring to the arbitrator's judgment on collective bargaining issues over which it would also have jurisdiction under the LMRA. The arbitrator's judgments on matters outside of NLRB statutory jurisdiction have remained sacrosanct and relatively unchallenged. A different situation has arisen under the rubric of enforcing public policy. Thus, an arbitrator might decide to return to work an employee discharged for using drugs, on the grounds that the employer had similarly treated other employees. However, such decisions are now more likely to be subject to judicial scrutiny on the merits and possibly be reversed on public policy grounds. The absence of any deferral process outside the LMRA tends to undercut the reputation of arbitration as a final and binding means of resolving collective bargaining disputes.

In an era of expanding legislative protection to employees, as in the field of discrimination law, arbitration could play a big role in relieving the courts of their burdens of review if arrangements could be made in which statutory agencies were willing to defer to arbitration, as does the NLRB, on statutory matters within their control. If such an arrangement could be put together, it would provide far greater authority to arbitrators in the nonunion sector than available to arbitrators in the collective bargaining sector.

Adaptability

Arbitration under collective agreements has given rise to an image of fairness, justice, and due process underscored by its acceptance by the courts as a credible societal institution for resolving disputes. The union-management arbitration system, with its standards of fairness and due process, may be particularly appealing to the courts. The system works, and ever-more-crowded criminal and drug dockets are leading the courts to seek ways to reduce their civil case backlogs. At the same time, however, the credibility of the union-management arbitration system has been adversely affected by some employers who apply the process to self-created systems that lack many of the fairness and due process components that have given arbitration its community credibility.

The requirements for equity and legal protection to our total workforce raise the question of whether the union-management system could be adapted to meet the needs of this substantially greater market. But this is a market without union parity or employee representation in developing such arbitration procedures. It is a market without a trained cadre of experienced arbitrators conversant with the requirements of the laws and the courts. It is a market where the government agencies have statutory and political obligations to fulfill, and where privatizing functions raises potential suspicions and territorial threats.

It is a market where the courts are concerned about losing jurisdiction at the same time they are pressured by increases in legislation, litigation, and backlogs of unresolved civil law cases. And finally it is a market where the employers currently have the authority to require new hires to agree to arbitrate disputes not readily foreseeable through a procedure the employers alone design and to which the courts defer.

It is not too much to expect that the benefits of the union-management arbitration system can be adapted to meet the needs of this bigger, doubting, and imbalanced market. There must be a way found to eliminate the inequities of the present nonunion employment law dispute resolution system and change it into one that replicates the due process standards of labor-management arbitration.

Summary

Over the decades, unions and management—with the eventual consent of government agencies and the courts—have crafted a structure for resolving disputes arising in the application of collective bargaining agreements. In the private sector the consequence of not following such systems was strike and lockout, with the obvious risk of loss of employment, income, and profit. In the public sector the consequence of not using a parallel system was the risk of violating laws against strikes by public employees as well as prolonged legal proceedings and intense political pressures. Thus in collective bargaining in both the public and private sectors, the parties have found it in their own interest to develop standards of fairness in their mutual quest to get disputes behind them so that operations may continue without interruption or distraction. The ad hoc resort to mediation and arbitration of interest issues and the near-universal use of mediation and arbitration for grievances has worked sufficiently well that both parties have been hard-pressed to find any mutually effective substitute.

Arbitration and mediation of union-management disputes has both advantages and disadvantages. There is no pretense that the procedures are a panacea for resolving all disputes outside the collective bargaining context. But—as the result of decades of collective bargaining and arbitration decisions—they do set forth standards for fair treatment and resolution of disputes. It is those standards of fairness and due process that should be worthy of general adoption if arbitration in the employment law arena is to treat employees and employers fairly and to bring greater equity to the resolution of workplace disputes.

Chapter Three

The Emergence of Alternative Dispute Resolution

The New Deal era witnessed a rapid expansion in the number of administrative agencies with jurisdiction over various aspects of business life. The Securities and Exchange Commission (SEC), the NLRB, and the Wage and Hour Administration joined those created earlier, such as the Interstate Commerce Commission and the Federal Trade Commission. Deep controversy arose over the nature of these agencies, their legitimate place in the American system of law and government, and the procedures under which they should operate—on the model of a court of law or as expert administrators with broad legislative mandates. The conflict was bitter at times.

James M. Landis, second Chairman of the SEC and "the outstanding theoretician of American regulation," held that the "administrative process springs from the inadequacy of a simple tripartite form of government [executive, legislative, judicial] to deal with modern problems."[1] Further, "the administrative process is, in essence, our generation's answer to the inadequacy of the judicial and the legislative process."[2] Opponents held that administrative agencies constituted a "headless fourth branch of the government" and did "violence to the basic theory of the American constitution that there should be three branches of government and only three."

President Roosevelt vetoed legislation in 1940 that would have prescribed for these agencies the rigid and formal rules of the courts. He stated: "[A] large part of the legal profession, has never reconciled itself to the existence of the administrative tribunal. Many of them prefer the stately ritual of the courts, in which lawyers play the speaking parts, to the simple procedure of administrative hearings which a client can understand and even participate in."[3] It was not until 1946 that the Administrative Procedures Act was enacted, prescribing procedures for rulemaking by administrative agencies; it was a compromise between plans proposed by the administration and the ABA. Tensions between formality and flexibility in the administrative processes of rulemaking and adjudication were built into the legislation.

This early struggle over the legitimacy of administrative agencies and their role in the American system of law and government was to be replicated in recent years as critics of the formality and delays of administrative agencies sought to develop rules and regulations by processes more informal, more rapid, and more responsive to the political process.

James Landis, in a report to President-elect Kennedy in 1960, "catalogued the breakdown of the system he had celebrated only twenty-two years earlier."[4] Although the 1930 reforms were aimed at efficiency, Landis held that by 1960 delays and backlogs had become the hallmark of federal regulation. His remedy was improved personnel—stronger powers for agency chairmen, higher salaries, and longer tenure. The Kennedy administration responded by making a number of new first-rate appointments.[5]

At about the same time, some professional economists launched a major attack on rate and price regulation in such industries as airlines, trucking, railroads, electric power, and communications. It took several decades, but this attack did eventually lead to substantial deregulation of the product markets of these sectors.[6]

Despite the massive pullback from product market regulation—including the demise of several specialized agencies—labor market regulation by federal and state governments has continued to expand. The widespread attention by economists and the equally widespread hostility by management groups to many labor market regulations has not led to any consensus either in professional or public opinion for wholesale deregulation of labor markets.[7] Attention to the regulatory process and to adjudication is accordingly the more imperative in labor markets.

It is useful to distinguish two complementary procedures within an agency in applying statutory enactments. There is the process of applying statutory law—as interpreted and defined by regulations issued by the designated agency—to individual cases or disputes, through an adjudicatory process potentially followed by resort to the courts. There is also the distinct process of formulating and issuing the detailed regulations themselves. These twin processes are somewhat analogous to the related activities under collective bargaining, identified in Chapter One, of the process of settling grievances by mediation or arbitration under an agreement and the process employed to reach the agreement in the first place.

Efforts to reform the regulatory process have been directed to both processes. Current statutes (1996) authorize ADR in resolving particular cases and negotiated rulemaking in establishing regulations. The two processes are interrelated; experience teaches that the more consensual the development process, the less extensive the litigation in the adjudication and application of the regulations and the statute.

This chapter is divided into three sections. It begins by discussing the difficulties with conventional adjudication of disputes under employment law, and then traces the development of ADR in adjudication. It concludes with the development of negotiated rulemaking.

Conventional Dispute Adjudication

Questions concerning the appropriate mechanisms for applying regulations and statutes to particular cases and for resolving disputes over their applications have become more insistent in the past decade. The traditional procedure has been to resort to diverse administrative steps and mechanisms provided in each statute—inspectors, regional offices, administrative determinations, administrative law judges, specialized tribunals—and then to address appeals to the regular federal courts.

Various forms of ADR have emerged in the past several decades, offering alternatives to the specified agency and court procedures for at least some types of adjudication of disputes under employment law. ADR methods may be used by specialized staff internal to an agency or by outside neutrals. The acronym ADR has come to refer to the following types of techniques in dispute resolution: arbitration, med-arb (mediation followed by arbitration), fact-finding, minitrial, neutral evaluation, mediation, facilitation, convening, conciliation, and negotiations.[8] Of this group, only arbitration and med-arb provide for a final and binding resolution. Accordingly, the present attention focuses on arbitration or med-arb.

The Labor Department is currently responsible for the administration of approximately 180 statutes[9] that can be labeled as employment law. This list has grown from the small numbers of the 1930s—through both Republican and Democratic administrations—to the present long list of complex legislation.[10] Employment law also includes the various programs designed to eliminate discrimination, which are administered by the EEOC and state agencies. In the broadest sense, employment law also includes workers' compensation and labor-management statutes, particularly the Labor-Management Relations Act (LMRA).

As noted in the Preface, the mission statement of the Commission on the Future of Worker-Management Relations (1993–1995) asked, "What, if anything, should be done to increase the extent to which work-place problems are resolved by the parties themselves, rather than by recourse to state and federal courts and government regulatory bodies?"

As in earlier periods, it now appears that widespread malaise and dissatisfaction characterizes the application of many of these statutes and regulations of employment law to individual situations and to the resolution of particular disputes involving workers, whether or not under collective bargaining, public and private managers, and the administrative agencies. To briefly summarize the major manifestations of these problems:

- There was more than a fourfold increase in employment law litigation (from 4,331 cases to almost 23,000 cases) in the federal courts between 1971 and 1991.[11] In the state courts, cases of wrongful dismissal have substantially increased.

- The funding of the administrative agencies has been constricted so that their investigative staffs have declined, and the general expectation is that prospective funding levels will require further staff reductions.[12]

- As a consequence, the backlog of cases in the agencies has grown substantially. By the end of 1995, for example, the EEOC reported an inventory of approximately a hundred thousand complaints.[13]

- A number of federal statutes since 1990 have sought to encourage resort to alternative methods of dispute resolution, but the response thus far has been minuscule on the part of all parties.[14]

- Protection for low-wage workers who lack representation is particularly constrained by the high costs and duration of litigation. Litigation to achieve statutory rights tends to be attempted much more by managerial and professional employees than by low-wage employees.

- Most employment discrimination suits are brought by employees who have already left the job where the complaint arose and who have little practical expectation of returning to the same workplace. At best the delayed processes provide damage awards to ex-employees rather than protection to current employees.

- In some highly competitive sectors, particularly those with high labor costs, widespread noncompliance results in uneven treatment of workers and unfair competitive advantages for violators—who thus undermine socially determined standards. (For example, consider the working conditions in some parts of the New York and Los Angeles women's garment industry.)

- A number of employer-initiated dispute resolution systems are being established in nonunion workplaces—often as a condition of employment—to respond to the growth in employment law litigation and to its costs. Serious issues arise as to the fairness and the due-process standards of arbitration under some of these plans.

- The courts have provided somewhat mixed and conflicting signals with respect to the status of private arbitration plans as applied to employment rights specified in public law. (See Chapter Four for a detailed discussion.) In the 1974 ruling mentioned in Chapter Two, *Alexander v. Gardner-Denver*, the Supreme Court ruled that a unionized employee with a racial discrimination claim was not bound nor required to have the claim disposed by an arbitrator under the collective bargaining agreement; the employee was free, instead, to pursue the case in federal court. No deferral to the collective bargaining agreement was required.

In the 1991 *Gilmer v. Interstate/Johnson Lane Corp.* ruling, the Supreme Court appeared to take a different direction. It decided that a nonunion employee was required to submit a claim of age discrimination to arbitration under the employee's securities industry agreement, which directed all such claims to a private arbitration system established by the employer. In that instance, the employee could not pursue the claim as a violation of the Age Discrimination in Employment Act. There is dispute over the reach and application of *Gilmer*.[15]

The Commission on the Future of Worker-Management Relations considered two broad and quite different approaches to enhance dispute resolution over the meaning and application of regulations of employment law. Either of these approaches could apply to a full range of procedures, whether developed by the traditional methods of the Administrative Procedures Act or by negotiated rulemaking. The radical approach would create a unified labor court system in this country comparable to those in a number of European countries and in some developing countries, as in Brazil. A more limited version would provide a single circuit court to decide cases arising from administrative agencies as was provided by statute for temporary wage and price controls between 1970 and 1974.

At the present time there are approximately twenty major adjudicatory procedures—and a considerable number of minor ones—in the Labor Department alone, arising from the separate accretion of employment statutes over the years. In this line of proposals, the Congress might establish for the Labor Department a single procedure, involving massive revisions in the adjudication provision of current employment statutes. The complexity of this approach is only one of its disadvantages, as it is difficult to picture a single procedure that would be entirely appropriate for all statutes from pension regulation to wage and hour cases.

The Commission therefore proposed a more limited and gradual revision of current practice by encouraging further experimentation by employers, administrative agencies, parties to collective agreements, and interest groups representing individual plaintiffs (civil rights, labor unions, and women's organizations) to adopt equitable and effective standards for voluntary mediation and arbitration in appropriate cases of disputes over employment rights.[16] (These standards are discussed in Chapter Four. Not all disputes over the application of statutory and administrative agency regulations are suitable for arbitration.)

The Development of ADR in Adjudication

Since the mid-1950s, the NLRB has applied a policy of deferral to arbitration awards under collective bargaining agreements involving a variety of statutory issues under the LMRA.[17] The agency has deferred to arbitration awards under an existing collective bargaining agreement where an unfair labor practice charge presenting a similar issue has been pending in a regional office or filed subsequent to the arbitration award. The scope of prearbitration deferral has varied over the years but has been applied to charges in a setting of an existing labor agreement and the availability of grievance-arbitration machinery.[18]

The Administrative Dispute Resolution Act of 1990[19] provided that each agency "shall adopt a policy that addresses the use of alternative means of dispute resolution and case management." In 1992 the Department of Labor experimented with the use of in-house mediators in cases involving OSHA and Wage-Hour violations awaiting litigation in the Philadelphia Region. Of the twenty-seven cases referred to mediation, twenty-two (81 percent) were settled, most in a single mediation session. Some of the cases were very complex and would have cost the Department and the outside parties substantial resources and time to litigate. The Department participants reported that the settlements were comparable to the likely outcome of litigation.[20] Despite these favorable results, however, the Department made no follow-up or general application.

In a pilot project and evaluation completed in 1994, the EEOC offered internal staff mediation that proved to be a successful program.[21] The average time for completion of the mediation process was 67 days—compared to 247 days under the standard investigatory process. In 1995 the EEOC made the mediation program a continuing feature of its administration, and on July 17 of that year the EEOC affirmed the agency's "commitment to using alternative dispute resolution (ADR) methods throughout its operations."[22] The Commission reiterated its long-standing opposition to preemployment agreements that mandate binding arbitration of discrimination disputes as a condition of employment. In 1996 the EEOC entered into an agreement with the FMCS for reimbursement to conduct a nationwide demonstration project on how to implement an external mediation program. The program included training in selected district offices. Charges referred for mediation were to be screened to conform to EEOC standards for cases to be mediated.[23]

The extent to which ADR methods are growing among private employers, outside of collective agreements and without sanction of the agencies administering statutes, is illustrated by a study of the U.S. General Accounting Office on employment discrimination.[24] Among enterprises with a hundred or more employees, almost all employers make use of one or more ADR approach; 10 percent use arbitration. Arbitration was mandatory for all covered employees in about one-fourth to one-half of those using arbitration. The GAO reported that a number of these arbitration plans would not meet the standards of due process and equity proposed by the Commission, however.

A significant development toward the implementation of arbitration of employment law disputes occurred in May 1995, with the issuance of the *Protocol* described in the Preface. (See Appendix B for the full text.) The *Protocol* was signed by individual officers of significant organizations involved in the adjudication of employment law disputes: the Council and the Arbitration Committee of the ABA Labor and Employment Section, the NAA, the AAA, the FMCS, the Workplace Rights Project of the ACLU, the Society of Professionals in Dispute Resolution, and the National Employment Lawyers Association.

Except on the issue of the requirement of arbitration as a condition of employment, on which the signatories to the *Protocol* were unable to agree, the due process statement prescribed in detail the standards, constraints, and limitations appropriate to arbitration of employment disputes involving statutory rights in work settings without collective bargaining agreements.

In a further extension of support for ADR in the resolution of statutory disputes arising out of the employment relationship, the Secretary of Labor's Task Force on Excellence in State and Local Government Through Labor-Management Cooperation advocated voluntary arbitration as a means to resolve disputes in the public sector. These disputes are governed by many of the same federal statutes and regulations as the private sector.[25] It also elaborated on the standards for effective ADR systems for rights guaranteed by public law advanced by the Commission and the *Protocol*.

On February 14, 1996, the Massachusetts Commission Against Discrimination issued the first set of agency regulations offering arbitration on a voluntary basis by outside neutrals to those seeking redress from employment-based discrimination.[26] (Chapter Eight discusses these regulations in detail, and Appendix C provides the full text.) Chairman Michael T. Duffy, influenced by the due process *Protocol*, had extended consultations with Massachusetts representatives for management and the plaintiff bar who together encouraged the development of the voluntary arbitration option.

The Development of Negotiated Rulemaking

The traditional regulatory process involves an administrative agency issuing a notice of a draft regulation, requesting detailed comments with briefs and in hearings, and eventually issuing a final rule—which is typically followed by litigation. By contrast, the basic idea of negotiated rulemaking is that "in certain situations it is possible to bring together representatives of the agency and the various interest groups to negotiate the text of a proposed rule."[27] The Administrative Procedures Act requires only that the agency publish any proposed rule and allow an opportunity for comment before final issuance.

A number of events in the mid-1970s advanced the development of negotiated rulemaking, and by a decade later it had become a recognized and legitimate method of promulgating regulations by administrative agencies generally, including those establishing rules under employment law, although the procedures continue to be infrequently used.

By 1975, the Department of Labor had been transformed into a conglomerate of major regulatory programs in employment law. "In 1940 the Department administered 18 regulatory programs; by

1960 the number had expanded to 40; in 1975, the number stands at 134."[28] Secretary Dunlop issued a memorandum to the staff pointing out that "a major reason for the attraction of regulation over the years has been the belief that it is a speedy, simple and cheap procedure. It should be apparent that the administrative procedure is by no means fast or inexpensive." The memorandum listed eleven problems with the then-current procedures and made six suggestions to make the regulatory process more responsive to the problems cited. The memorandum concluded with these observations:

> The country needs to acquire a more realistic understanding of the limitations on bringing about social change through legal compulsion. A great deal of government time needs to be devoted to improving understanding, persuasion, accommodation, mutual problem solving, and informal mediation.
>
> The development of new attitudes on the part of public employees and new relationships and procedures with those who are required to live under regulations is a central challenge of democratic society. Trust cannot grow in an atmosphere dominated by bureaucratic fiat and litigious controversy; it emerges through persuasion, mutual accommodation, and problem solving.[29]

The memorandum proposed that "the parties who will be affected by a set of regulations should be involved to a greater extent in developing those regulations." The idea of negotiated rulemaking was applied by the Secretary to two rules as an experiment in seeking consensus among the major affected parties on rules to be published in the *Federal Register* for full general comment. One selected regulation concerned Section 13(c) of the Urban Mass Transportation Act, providing that subsidy funding require the Secretary of Labor to certify that employees not be adversely affected by federal funded activities, and the other concerned the health and safety standards for employees on coke ovens under OSHA.[30]

At about the same time, Richard B. Stewart explored systematically possible alternative procedures available to administrative agencies in promulgating rules. He regarded traditional procedural frameworks as seriously flawed, and he explored more "explicitly political" mechanisms for interest representation.[31] "Increasingly the function of administrative law is not the protection of private autonomy but the provision of a surrogate political process to ensure the fair representation of a wide range of affected interests in the process of administrative decision."[32] Further, Frank E. A. Sander presented an influential paper at the 1976 Pound Conference.[33]

The work of Philip J. Harter and the Administrative Conference of the United States (ACUS) developed these ideas and beginnings into operationally endorsed procedures.[34] Harter also drafted ACUS Recommendation 82–4, which provided recommended regulations for agencies considering the use of regulatory negotiations.[35] Chief Justice Burger delivered an address in this vein titled "Isn't There a Better Way."[36]

In three years after the adoption of ACUS Recommendation 82–4, negotiated rulemaking was employed four times by federal agencies—once by OSHA, once by the Federal Aviation Administration, and twice by the Environmental Protection Agency.[37] The experience in agencies that have conducted negotiations to formulate regulations is that subsequent litigation over the rules is almost eliminated. ACUS Recommendation 85–5 concluded that negotiated rulemaking was a viable and practical alternative to the notice-and-comment process of the Administrative Procedures Act and offered guidance as to how agencies and private participants could increase the prospects of reaching a consensus. Of course, negotiated rulemaking is not appropriate for all rules under a statute—but it is very effective when used selectively.

A more recent experience is provided by the OSHA steel erection standard. "For years the National Erectors Association and the Iron Workers International Union had urged the Department of Labor to approve negotiated rule-making to resolve profound differences between the industry and the government. Finally in 1994, DOL approved the industry's request."[38] The rulemaking advisory committee included representatives of three contractor associations, including union and nonunion contractors, as well as representatives of two very different unions. Philip J. Harter was the facilitator. The advisory committee reached consensus on the text of a proposed rule in December 1995 after eleven meetings. The committee crafted several provisions responsive to the concerns of small erectors. As OSHA Assistant Secretary Dear testified, "Past experience has taught us that negotiated rulemaking is advantageous only when all major interests in a particular rulemaking are represented, and when the issues addressed are finite and manageable within the available time. If not, there is almost a guarantee that the final rule will end up in litigation."[39] The final drafting of the regulations has been held up by DOL lawyers, but the regulation for practical purposes is largely in effect.

A central difficulty with the Administrative Procedures Act, particularly in the employment law field, is that agency regulators draft rules, publish them in the *Federal Register*, hold hearings and receive comments, and then issue final regulations with no direct participation of the parties who will be required to live under the rules, and with no opportunity for direct interaction among the affected parties over the proposed rule. The comments often present extreme views and legal arguments of the most concerned parties and their biased versions of the facts. The scene is set for extended litigation on the legislation and what the regulations mean in the finest detail.[40] Negotiated rulemaking emerged in reaction to the unsuitability of notice-and-comment procedures for making quasi-legislative decisions. This development is analogous to the enactment of the Administrative Procedures Act of 1946 as a reaction against courtlike procedures for setting regulations in administrative agencies.

The process of negotiated rulemaking, developed as briefly described in this section, was fully endorsed and authorized by the Negotiated Rulemaking Act of 1990[41] and reaffirmed by the

Administrative Dispute Resolution Act of 1996.[42] The formal procedures of the 1946 Administrative Procedures Act now have a more informal legitimate alternative to take into account a variety of constituencies and interests in issuing regulations under federal employment law.

Summary

Somewhat analogous to the distinction made in Chapter One between disputes over the terms of a collective bargaining agreement and those over the meaning and application of an agreement, this chapter developed the distinction between controversies over the process of determining administrative agency regulations under a statute and the process of adjudicating or applying a rule to particular cases or disputes.

The adjudication of disputes over the application of rules by ADR processes has only begun on a trial basis in a few programs. Despite the success of arbitration in both the private and public sectors under collective bargaining, despite the formal recommendations of bodies of experts and the authorization of Congress, and despite the growing resort to arbitration of statutory disputes arising out of the employment relations in a growing number of businesses—albeit some with dubious standards—administrative agencies have only begun to consider policies in this area. But the course of preferred future developments is sketched in the chapters that follow.

The process of establishing rules by administrative agencies in the 1930s was controversial, with some arguing that these agencies should function like a court and others describing the proper role as governed by expertise but insulated from political control. The Administrative Procedures Act of 1946 had elements of both views. The process of consult, publish in the *Federal Register*, consult, publish in final form—and then litigate in the courts—led to what Philip J. Harter called a malaise in which parties complained about the time, expense, and practicality of the procedures. Negotiated rulemaking, which began in the mid-1970s, was authorized in 1990 by statute and reaffirmed in 1996 as an appropriate and legitimate alternative. To date, however, the process has been used only infrequently by employment law agencies in setting rules.

The application of statutes and regulations to individual cases is facilitated—made less litigious and more amenable to mediation and arbitration—when the regulations have been established by negotiated rulemaking. The 1996 statute, recognizing their interdependency, revalidated both ADR methods of adjudication and negotiated rulemaking to establish regulations.

Chapter Four

The Current State of Employment Law Arbitration

The current state of employment law relative to the arbitration of statutory disputes is comparable to water running in two streams that merge into a single river. The two parallel streams have been arbitration under collective bargaining agreements and arbitration of commercial disputes. In the collective bargaining arena, grievance and arbitration provisions for resolving midcontract disputes received endorsement by the Supreme Court as enforceable contracts in the 1960 *Steelworkers Trilogy*. In the commercial sector the endorsement of arbitration arose as a function of commercial contract enforcement, traditionally negotiated by the commercial partners to resolve internal disputes without resort to litigation.

The separate traditions of each stream are understandable in light of their respective histories. But these traditions and their respective standards are becoming blurred as the traditional commercial arbitration structures are expanded to deal with employment issues. Society now has a growing interest in arbitration as the faster, more economical, and preferred means of resolving employment disputes, particularly as they concern rights protected by state and federal statutes.

This chapter traces the two streams with attention to extending the due process protections so carefully developed for collective-bargaining arbitration and commercial disputes into the new and expanding field of individual employment disputes. It is reasonable to anticipate that statutory arbitration will increasingly provide assurances of due process and fairness. The question is when and how.

This chapter is divided into two sections. The first traces the development of finality of arbitration under collective bargaining agreements and the second does the same for employment law arbitration outside the union-management field.

Collective Bargaining Agreements

The Steelworkers Trilogy

The 1960 rulings of the Supreme Court in the *Steelworkers Trilogy* cases marked a culmination of years of growing respect for the self-regulation of unions and management in monitoring conduct of the parties under collective bargaining.[1] In 1947, the LMRA granted jurisdiction to the federal courts to handle suits for violation of contracts between labor organizations and employers, permitting labor organizations to sue and be sued.[2] In 1954, Harvard law professor Archibald Cox in a landmark article urged legal sanctions be added to economic power for enforcement of agreements.[3] In 1957, Mr. Justice Douglas for the Supreme Court in *Lincoln Mills*[4] accepted the view that "the agreement to arbitrate grievance disputes is the quid pro quo for an agreement not to strike," and that Section 301 of LMRA "expresses a federal policy that federal courts should enforce these agreements on behalf of or against labor organizations and that industrial peace can be best obtained only in that way."

In 1960 Mr. Justice Douglas wrote the three decisions that make up the historic *Steelworkers Trilogy*. In *Warrior and Gulf*[5] he stated:

> In the commercial case, arbitration is the substitute for litigation. Here arbitration is the substitute for industrial strife. Since arbitration of labor disputes has quite different functions from arbitration under an ordinary commercial agreement, the hostility evinced by the courts toward arbitration of commercial agreements has no place here. For arbitration of labor disputes under collective bargaining agreements is part and parcel of the collective bargaining

process itself. . . . The collective agreement covers the whole employment relationship. It calls into being a new common law— the common law of a particular industry or of a particular plant. . . . A collective bargaining agreement is an effort to erect a system of industrial self-government.

Adopting the reasoning of Yale law professor Harry Shulman,[6] the Court held that the labor-management arbitrator performs functions and fashions judgments "that may indeed be foreign to the competence of courts." It added:

The labor arbitrator is usually chosen because of the parties' confidence in his knowledge of the common law of the shop and their trust in his personal judgment to bring to bear considerations which are not expressed in the contract as criteria for judgment. . . . For the parties' objective in using the arbitration process is primarily to further their common goal of uninterrupted production under the agreement, to make the agreement serve their specialized needs. The ablest judge cannot be expected to bring the same experience and competence to bear upon the determination of a grievance because he cannot be similarly informed.

The Court went on to restrict inquiry to the question of whether the parties agreed to arbitrate a grievance or give the arbitrator the power to make an award, noting that: "An order to arbitrate the particular grievance should not be denied unless it may be said with positive assurance that the arbitration clause is not susceptible to an interpretation that covers the asserted dispute. Doubts should be resolved in favor of coverage."

In *American Manufacturing*,[7] the court went further to hold that it should not determine whether the moving party is right or wrong, since that is a question for the arbitrator to determine, noting that the moving party should not be deprived of the arbitrator's judgment because that is what the parties bargained for in agreeing to arbitration. Arbitration is thus available for all grievances, and not merely those the court deems meritorious. "The processing of even frivolous claims may have therapeutic values of which those who are not a part of the plant environment may be quite unaware."

The first two cases of the *Trilogy* concerned arbitrability. The third, *Enterprise Wheel*,[8] focused on the substantive authority of the arbitrator. It prescribed the circumstances when a court can overturn an arbitrator's award that is not based on the parties' agreement: "An arbitrator is expected to render an informed judgment to reach a fair solution even in the area of remedies. Nevertheless, an arbitrator is confined to interpretation and application of the collective bargaining agreement; he does not sit to dispense his own brand of industrial justice. He may of course look for guidance from many sources, yet his award is legitimate only so long as it draws its essence from the collective bargaining agreement. When the arbitrator's words manifest an infidelity to this obligation, courts have no choice but to refuse enforcement of the award."

Following these decisions, labor and management did not recoil from arbitration. They continued to rely upon it in virtually all collective bargaining agreements as the preferred procedure for resolving disputes over the meaning and application of the agreements in the organized sector. Indeed, the *Steelworkers Trilogy* was heralded as opening the Golden Age of Arbitration.

Arbitration of Statutory Law

The strong endorsement of union-management arbitration by the Court led to a vigorous debate among scholars on the extent of the arbitrator's authority, particularly in regard to statutory matters. Was the arbitrator confined to contractual matters? What if the parties incorporated into their agreement a provision requiring compliance with a statute? Certainly the Court had given the arbitrator authority over the content of the contract. But are employees who otherwise would have access to statutory rights deprived of that access to the administrative agencies and the courts when the parties grant to an arbitrator the authority to determine those statutory rights?

In a series of cases, the NLRB considered the conflict between its own authority to administer the LMRA and its endorsement of arbitration as the preferred procedure for resolving workplace disputes. What if an employee who was terminated by the employer for poor workmanship claimed the termination was not for poor workmanship but for union activity, otherwise protected under Sec 8(a)(3) of the LMRA? The Board has followed a dual route on deferral. It has developed procedures that attempt to give full faith and credit to the decisions of arbitrators selected by the parties within their collective bargaining structure. In doing so it also recognized the qualifications of the arbitrator selected by the parties to hear, weigh, and decide the issues giving rise to the unfair labor-practice charge.

On cases that come to it through its own complaint procedures, commencing with the *Collyer* case in 1971,[9] the Board took the position that where there was a statutory as well as an arbitrable issue, it would refrain from processing the complaint, but retain jurisdiction of the case until it could examine the decision of the arbitrator on the contractual issue.

The more recent approach to dual jurisdiction taken by the NLRB has been to examine its statutory responsibility *following* the issuance of the arbitration award, to see if that statutory obligation has been recognized in the decision of the arbitrator. The landmark case on this subject has led to the establishment of what is called the *Spielberg*[10] Doctrine. Under that concept the Board defers to a prior arbitrator's decision if the arbitration proceedings were fair and regular, if the parties agreed to be bound by the arbitrator's decision, and if the arbitration award was not clearly repugnant to the purposes and policies of the LMRA. After several turns in subsequent cases, the Board reaffirmed *Spielberg* in 1984 in its *Olin*[11] decision. Reiterating the *Spielberg* standards, the Board went on: "And with regard to the inquiry into the clearly repugnant standard, we would not require an arbitrator's award to be totally consistent with Board precedent. Unless the award is 'palpably wrong,' i.e., unless the arbitrator's decision is not susceptible to an interpretation consistent with the Act, we will defer." Furthermore, the burden on such cases would be on the party seeking to have the Board ignore the arbitrator's determination.

The referral concept has been effective where there is in place a collective bargaining agreement calling for arbitration of the issues giving rise to the charges brought to the NLRB. But what about charges of unfair labor practices in enterprises where there is no collective bargaining agreement? Could arbitration developed by the employer without a collective bargaining agreement be made available to the charging employee to be invoked to resolve those issues in similar fashion?

Such accommodation to arbitration by a federal agency might prove a viable standard for handling other statutory issues. Understandably, the NLRB is sufficiently supportive of arbitration under collective bargaining agreements to defer to duly appointed arbitrators' decisions even in matters embracing its statutory responsibility. But the NLRB, after all, bears responsibility for enforcing that same statute that gives rise to the credibility of arbitration as the forum of preference in resolving workplace disputes. But would the NLRB be willing to defer to the decision of an arbitrator selected under an employer-promulgated system imposed on an employee as a condition of hire or continued employment? Unfortunately, no other administrative agency has been so forthcoming in respecting the statutory judgments of arbitrators.

Beyond the LMRA the debate has raged on. It was initially manifest in a series of papers presented before the National Academy of Arbitrators in 1967. Professor Bernard Meltzer[12] took the position that where there was an irrepressible conflict between the law and the agreement, the arbitrator should ignore the law. Arbitrator Robert Howlett[13] took the opposite view. He held that arbitrators should render decisions based on contract and law, noting that, like judges, arbitrators are subject to and bound by laws, federal, state, and local, and that all contracts—including collective bargaining agreements—are subject to, and indeed include, all applicable law, statute as well as the common law of the jurisdiction in which they were crafted.

The issue of the arbitrator's authority to bind the parties to an award applying or denying application of a statute (other than the LMRA) was brought to the Supreme Court in 1974 and decided in the case of *Alexander* v. *Gardner-Denver*.[14] There the parties' agreement prohibited discrimination based on race, and prohibited termination unless for "just cause." Alexander, a black, was terminated for poor work performance. He filed a grievance with the union, as well as a claim with the state agency alleging racial discrimination in his termination as a violation of Title VII of the Civil Rights Act. In arbitration his termination was found to be for just cause. The Federal District Court dismissed the case, accepting the arbitrator's decision as binding on Alexander, and the Court of Appeals confirmed the dismissal. The Supreme Court reversed the Court of Appeals, finding that since the agreement contained a discrimination ban, the arbitrator's decision did not dispose of the statutory issue. The Court highlighted the separate nature of the contractual and statutory rights, noting that the LMRA did not bar the NLRB from considering a claimed violation of that statute, even though ruled on by the arbitrator. Although it recognized there could be prospective waiver of collective statutory rights under a collective labor agreement, the rights protected by Title VII were "an individual's right to equal employment opportunities." Title VII constitutes a "Congressional command that each employee be free from discriminatory practices . . . [a right] not susceptible of prospective waiver." Relying on *Steelworkers* v. *Enterprise Wheel and Car Corporation*, the Court noted that an arbitrator is confined to the interpretation and application of the agreement, and that an arbitrator's "award is legitimate only as long as it draws its essence from the collective bargaining agreement," and added that "where the collective bargaining agreement conflicts with Title VII, the arbitrator must follow the agreement."

The Court found arbitration to be "comparatively inferior to judicial processes in the protection of Title VII rights." In the oft-quoted footnote 21, the Court held:

> We adopt no standards as to the weight to be accorded an arbitral decision, since this must be determined in the court's discretion with regard to the facts and circumstances of each case. Relevant factors include the existence of provisions in the collective bargaining agreement that conform substantially to Title VII, the degree of procedural fairness in the arbitral forum, adequacy of the record with respect to the issue of discrimination and the special competence of particular arbitrators. Where an arbitral determination gives full consideration to an employee's Title VII rights, a court may properly accord it great weight. . . . But courts should ever be mindful that Congress, in enacting Title VII, thought it necessary to provide a judicial forum for the ultimate resolution of discriminatory employment claim. It is the duty of courts to assure the full availability of this forum.

Since 1974 *Alexander* v. *Gardner-Denver* has continued to be the law of the land, barring arbitration under collective bargaining agreements of claimed statutory violations. The courts appear to adhere to the view that an employee will not be compelled to arbitrate statutory issues where the parties' agreement is silent on arbitration of such issues. There are different views among the courts on whether arbitration may be compelled where the collective agreement provides for arbitration of statutory claims.

The collective bargaining agreement in *Alexander* v. *Gardner-Denver* barred discrimination, but did not authorize the arbitrator to resolve claims that related to specific statutory rights. Given the more recent rulings of the Supreme Court, one might expect that if a collective agreement did authorize the arbitrator to resolve disputes arising over claims of violation of the Civil Rights Act of 1991, that the Court might now have a different view of the finality of the arbitrator's decision.

Arbitration Outside the Union-Management Field

The question looms as to the status of arbitration of employment law issues outside the field of collective bargaining. Do the same rules of statutory jurisdiction apply in nonunion situations as under *Alexander v. Gardner-Denver* for employment under collective agreements? One might have thought so from the wording of Section One of the Federal Arbitration Act: "nothing herein contained shall apply to contracts of employment of seamen, railroad employees or any other class of workers engaged in foreign or interstate commerce."[15] But the Court in the *Gilmer*[16] case indicated a change to judicial deferral to arbitration in employment law in nonunion settings.

The history of Section 1 of the Federal Arbitration Act[17] does not refer to arbitration under collective bargaining agreements. Its language arose from a 1921 ABA draft federal arbitration act designed to reduce the delays of litigation and congestion in federal and state courts.[18] During Senate hearings on the bill in 1923, Andrew Furuseth, president of the International Seamen's Union (ISU), is cited as having objected to the proposed bill on the grounds that it would compel arbitration, and thus permit specific performance of the individually executed contracts of employment between stevedores and their employers, long objected to by the union. For stevedores in foreign ports such specific performance might be viewed as a "shanghai." The proponent of the bill, W.H.H. Piatt, stated, "It was not the intention of this bill to make an industrial arbitration in any sense,"[19] and proposed an insertion, noting that, "it is not intended that this be an act referring to labor disputes, at all. It is an act to give the merchants the right or privilege of sitting down and agreeing with each other as to what their damages are, if they want to do it."[20] He then proposed the following exemption: "but nothing herein contained shall apply to seamen or any class of workers of interstate and foreign commerce."

Thereafter with the consent of the ISU and the American Federation of Labor, the Federal Arbitration Act became law with the primary objective of expediting commerce, resolving commercial disputes, and avoiding the delays of litigation. The ancillary debate over the Section 1 exclusion was resolved by inserting the quoted exemption as proposed by then Secretary of Commerce Herbert Hoover, as a means of overcoming the objection "to the inclusion of worker's contracts in the law's scheme."[21]

In their interpretations of Section 1, the circuit courts had not applied the exemption broadly to apply to all employees in interstate commerce, whether under individual or collective agreements. Rather, as typified by the decision of the Third Circuit in its 1953 *Tenney Engineering*[22] decision, they sought to restrict the exemption to "only those other classes of workers who are actually engaged in the movement of interstate or foreign commerce or in work so closely related thereto as to be in practical effect part of it. The draftsmen had in mind the two groups of transportation workers as to which special arbitration legislation already existed and they rounded out the exclusionary clause by excluding all other similar classes of workers."

With this background, and amid a conflict between the circuits as to whether or not arbitration could be compelled in employment claims such as those alleging age discrimination, the *Gilmer* case came before the Supreme Court in 1991.[23] Robert Gilmer was a securities representative registered with the New York Stock Exchange under a National Association of Securities Dealers Form U–4 registration arrangement that committed him to arbitrate "any dispute, claim or controversy" arising between him and his employer. When he was terminated at age sixty-two he filed an age discrimination claim with the EEOC, and later sued contending his termination violated the Age Discrimination in Employment Act (ADEA). His employer sought to force him into arbitration in lieu of litigation. In the decision, Justice White for the majority found that Gilmer was compelled to arbitrate the age discrimination claim under the Stock Exchange arbitration scheme to which he had agreed at hire, even though the registration arrangement made no specific reference to arbitrating disputes covered by employment statutes or to the ADEA. The Court declined to interpret the Section 1 exception on the grounds that the petitioner had not raised that issue in the lower court proceedings, and that the arbitration clause occurred within a securities registration form rather than an employment contract. Justice Stevens in his dissent took the position that Section 1 of the Federal Arbitration Act covered all employment agreements.

The Court endorsed the role of the Federal Arbitration Act in seeking to "reverse the long-standing judicial hostility to arbitration agreements that had existed at English Common law and had been adopted by American courts, and to place arbitration agreements upon the same footing as other contracts." It found that statutory claims were properly subject to arbitration agreements, that there was nothing in the ADEA precluding arbitration, and that arbitration was not inconsistent with the ADEA. It reiterated its "current strong endorsement of the federal statutes favoring this method of resolving disputes."

The Court dismissed the speculation that arbitration panels would be biased, that discovery would not be as broad as in the federal courts, that the arbitrators might not issue written opinions, and that there would be unequal bargaining power between employers and employees. It asserted that the New York Stock Exchange arbitration rules provided adequate procedural protection for employees like Gilmer.

The Court's discussion of *Alexander v. Gardner-Denver* is hailed as establishing the primacy of the Federal Arbitration Act endorsement of predispute arbitration for resolving statutory issues, even though in 1974 it reserved to the courts the statutory decision-making authority when reviewing collective bargaining arbitration awards. It distinguished *Alexander v. Gardner-Denver* as restricting a labor arbitrator's "authority to resolve only questions of contractual rights," while lacking the "general authority to invoke public laws that conflict with the bargain between the parties." It also noted that in *Alexander v. Gardner-Denver* there was no "issue of the enforceability of an agreement to arbitrate statutory claims," no authorization for the arbitrators to decide statutory issues, and no coverage of the Federal Arbitration Act, which reflects a "liberal federal policy favoring arbitration agreements."

In footnote 5, the *Gilmer* Court did disavow its 1974 view of the arbitral process as "inferior to the judicial process for resolving statutory claims," noting that "that mistrust of the arbitral process however, has been undermined by our recent arbitration decisions."

But notwithstanding the failure to deal with the employment exclusion of Section 1, the Court made *Gilmer* the law of the land, endorsing contractually mandated arbitration of employment disputes. The *Gilmer* decision has been followed by the lower courts as strongly endorsing arbitration of employment disputes. There remain a number of questions that require examination.

Gilmer's *Impact on Employment Contracts*

The Supreme Court found that Gilmer was bound by the security registration agreement he signed at the time of employment. Accordingly it did not resolve the question of whether he would have been equally bound under an arbitration agreement that was specifically limited to employment issues, which would have more directly faced the Section 1 exemption. Nor did it resolve the question of whether Section 1 exempts only transportation and actual interstate movements of commerce—or whether it exempts interstate commerce as perceived in 1923 or as currently interpreted by the courts. The Sixth Circuit in *Asplundh Tree Expert Co.* v. *Bates*[24] narrowly construed the exclusion "to apply to employment contracts of seamen, railroad workers and any other class of workers actually engaged in the movement of goods in interstate commerce in the same way that seamen and railroad workers are."

Gardner-Denver was not specifically overruled by the Supreme Court in *Gilmer*. But a Fourth Circuit decision in March 1996 raised anew questions of *Alexander* v. *Gardner-Denver's* viability. In *Austin* v. *Owens-Brockway Glass Container, Inc.*,[25] Linda Austin sued in the District Court alleging violations of Title VII and the

Americans with Disabilities Act. The district court had granted the employer summary judgment "because she failed to submit her claim to mandatory arbitration under a collective bargaining agreement." The Fourth Circuit affirmed, holding in part that "the arbitration provisions in the collective bargaining agreement are obligatory and not permissive." The court went on: "As we have just demonstrated above, the collective bargaining agreement specifically provides for final and binding arbitration on account of each complaint asserted here: Title VII for the gender claim. And in part IIB, we have decided that such arbitration is obligatory, not discretionary."

In a perceptive dissent Judge Hall reminds the majority that "a labor union may not prospectively waive a member's individual right to choose a judicial forum for a statutory claim." Citing the unanimous ruling of the Supreme Court in *Alexander* v. *Gardner-Denver*, Judge Hall reasoned: "that a person may sue under Title VII not withstanding that he has submitted his claims to arbitration under a collective bargaining agreement and lost. In reaching this conclusion the Court stated that an employee's individual statutory right is completely independent of any contractual right he may have under a collective bargaining agreement, and the individual rights of employees are not subject to waiver by the union."

Judge Hall noted that in *Gilmer*, the Court "enforced an agreement to arbitrate contained in an individual (not collective) contract between a stockbroker and his employer. . . . Although (Justice White) eschewed language that expressed judicial mistrust of arbitration, he left its holding intact. He explained that the collective bargaining agreements of *Gardner-Denver* and its progeny did not contain the agreement of employees to arbitrate statutory claims. Second and of central importance here, because labor arbitrations involve contracts negotiated by unions, 'an important concern therefore was the tension between collective representation and individual statutory rights, a concern not applicable to the present case.' Finally, *Gilmer*, unlike the labor cases, arose under the Federal Arbitration Act."

Although the Supreme Court denied certiorari in *Owens-Brockway*, the incompatibility between the two Supreme Court cases remains to be resolved. Absent resolution we face a truly ironic situation: Professional arbitrators of collective bargaining disputes are barred from rendering statutory interpretations, even though they are bound by a code of ethical standards and have achieved respect for their competence and judgment by the parties' continued reliance on their decisions. Meanwhile, those designated as arbitrators under employer-promulgated schemes do have the authority to bind employees not covered by collective bargaining agreements to decisions on statutory issues, even though these so-called arbitrators have no such objective standards and perhaps even have no arbitral or statutory experience.

Statutory Authorization Under a Collective Agreement

Another unresolved question is whether an arbitrator selected and serving pursuant to the procedures of a collective bargaining agreement could be authorized by the parties to interpret and apply statutes. In *Alexander v. Gardner-Denver* the Court decision was based in part on the fact that the parties had not specifically submitted to the arbitrator jurisdiction over the ADEA. One wonders whether the "anti-arbitration" decision in *Alexander v. Gardner-Denver* might be squared with the deference to arbitration of statutory issues by the expedient of specific statutory reference in collective bargaining agreement arbitration submissions. Even though collective bargaining arbitrators lack the full range of statutory remedies, so too do may arbitrators under *Gilmer*. Recognizing such arbitration decisions would at least extend the endorsement of arbitration to the union sector, which has long advocated the practice even though it has been accorded second class standing for union members compared to its status in nonunion employment law disputes.

If *Gilmer* is to be followed rather than *Alexander* in the collective bargaining context, it raises even more issues. What is the impact on the traditional role of the NLRB in examining arbitration awards to determine if they are in compliance with the LMRA under the *Spielberg-Olin* deferral policy? Further, would following *Gilmer* mean that the arbitrator had immunity from judicial scrutiny of awards on public policy grounds, or would it maintain the traditional authority of the courts to resolve issues of substantive jurisdiction? Would the right to arbitrate a claim of statutory violation vest in the employee or remain as it is under most collective bargaining agreements within the province of the union? Would it become a violation of the duty of fair representation for a union to refuse to process—and fund—an employee's appeal of a statutory issue to arbitration?

Knowing and Voluntary Agreements to Arbitrate

A further unresolved question is the viability of holding that employees are bound by arbitration agreements signed at the time of, or even as a condition of, hire or continued employment. This of course has raised questions of whether arbitration agreements signed at the time of employment, well before any statutory violation might be perceived or even anticipated, can be described as knowing or voluntary.

Subsequent decisions have shed some light on those questions. In the *Prudential*[26] case in 1994, the Ninth Circuit took the position that an employee was not required to arbitrate a sex discrimination claim under a securities exchange registration agreement since neither the registration agreement nor the exchange rules referred to employment disputes. The court thus held that an employee is only barred from pursuing statutory appeals if the employee "knowingly agreed to submit such disputes to arbitration." But that reasoning—while extending the right to know the category of the subsequent dispute and employment issue—does not address the right to know the more important issue of whether an action may have violated a specific employment law. Extending the requirement of knowing to the generic employment category provides some protection but still does not run to the more relevant standard of whether an employee was willing to arbitrate alleged violations of specific statutes.

In *Williams v. Cigna Financial Advisors*[27] the Fifth Circuit held that the Older Workers Benefit Protection Act, which required written "knowing and voluntary" waiver of claims, did not preclude an agreement to initiate employment disputes, since that constituted a substitution of forum rather than a waiver of substantive rights or claims. There remain a number of other questions that require examination.

The issue of whether such preemployment signing is really voluntary when the job depends upon it is still a matter of dispute. Most district and circuit courts have embraced the *Gilmer* decision as requiring arbitration under such preemployment agreements. They have also held that other discrimination statutes such as Title VII are similar to the ADEA for purposes of compulsory arbitration.

One of the unresolved questions is whether a requirement to arbitrate established as a condition of employment is in fact a *contract of adhesion*. Such contracts—where one party imposes a contract that is outside the reasonable expectation of the weaker party, is unconscionable, or is offered on a take-it-or-leave-it basis— would be viewed as unenforceable even under *Gilmer*. The courts since *Gilmer* have declined to hold that preemployment obligations to arbitrate are in fact contracts of adhesion, but have recognized their potential in this context. Perhaps a stronger case can be made against a requirement of signing such commitments to arbitration as a condition of *continued* employment. That requirement is usually imposed on people who are already on the job when the employer introduces the new system or changes the system. The requirement of accepting those new restrictions or leaving the enterprise altogether appears even more onerous than requiring signing by new hires who have not yet committed their work lives to the establishment.

The *Gilmer* case arose prior to the commencement of the arbitration called for under the Form U–4. One wonders whether the court would rule as strongly in support of the employer-created structure if the arbitration had been fraught with due process irregularities, if there had been no reference to any statutory standards or protections in the decision, or if the employer's scheme had prohibited the arbitrator from granting punitive damages, or if the arbitrator was selected through a biased procedure or had demonstrated bias in the conduct of the hearing.

Positions on Mandatory Arbitration

Both the EEOC and the NLRB have challenged arbitration agreements imposed on employees before a dispute arises. On April 25, 1995, the EEOC stated its "opposition to agreements as a condition of initial or continued employment that mandate binding arbitration of employment discrimination disputes,"[28] adding that it would receive and process statutory charges regardless of the existence of an employer-sponsored ADR program. In the *River Oaks*[29] case, it obtained a permanent injunction against an employer who required employees to sign arbitration agreements after twenty-one employees had filed EEOC complaints and who retaliated against employees for filing with the EEOC. In that case the employer was enjoined from requiring employees: "to enter into any ADR policy which would cause an employee to pay the costs of ADR proceedings, [or] preclude or interfere with any employee's right to file complaints with the EEOC or to promptly file suit in a court of law when the employee has complied with the requirements of Title VII."

The general counsel NLRB has taken a similar position, charging that the discharge of employees under a mandatory arbitration system can constitute an unfair labor practice.[30] The issue is pending before the board.

These two positions are consistent with the *Report and Recommendations* of the Commission on the Future of Worker-Management Relations, and *Working Together for Public Service*[31] from the U.S. Secretary of Labor's Task Force on Excellence in State and Local Government Through Labor-Management Cooperation. Both called for arbitration of statutory disputes only on a postdispute basis. That position has also been espoused by National Employment Lawyers Association, the organization of the plaintiff bar. On May 21, 1997, the NAA adopted guidelines stating it "opposes mandatory employment arbitration as a condition of employment when it requires waiver of direct access to either a judicial or administrative forum for the pursuit of statutory rights."[32]

One would hope that the courts will become more critical in their support for employer-promulgated arbitration, if only to the extent of endeavoring to bolster the due process protections assumed by the Supreme Court in its decision in the *Gilmer* case. The mandatory predispute requirement of employer-promulgated arbitration may be efficient and may be replete with efforts to replicate the due process of administrative and judicial appeals, but the comparison fails when one considers that these alleged agreements are imposed as a condition of hire or of continued employment. Certainly candidates or employees may voluntarily decline the opportunity to take or remain in a job rather than accept the arbitration system. But to ascribe the term *voluntary* to people who need jobs ignores the economic reality of employment or the general tendency to think wishfully that a job will run smoothly and never lead to any conflict—particularly over external statutory rights. It is not at all unreasonable for job applicants to assume that even if they sign up to arbitrate any employment-related dispute, they will still have their rights as citizens to invoke protective statutes, to seek recourse through the courts, and perhaps enjoy the protections of the Seventh Amendment through trial by jury.

To underscore the deprivation of rights associated with mandatory arbitration is to recognize that the new employee—having signed the arbitration agreement to secure the job—has in effect waived any future rights to employment law protection even under laws not yet enacted. A final testament to the unilateral power of the employer in such structures is the right of the employer to amend or to dissolve the system. The employee has no such comparable right or authority and raises the risk of the employer unilaterally withdrawing the arbitration program if an effort is made to improve its impact on the employee.

Impact on Statutes Other Than ADEA

Since *Gilmer*, a number of courts have enforced arbitration agreements involving other discrimination statutes. In *Alford v. Dean Witter Reynolds*[33] and *Metz v. Merrill, Lynch, Pierce, Fenner and Smith, Inc.*[34] it was held to apply to claims arising under Title VII. In *Pritzker v. Merrill, Lynch, Pierce, Fenner and Smith, Inc.*[35] it was held to apply to a dispute arising under the Employee Retirement Income Security Act. It has also been applied to the Employee Polygraph Protection Act, the Equal Pay Act, the Racketeer Influenced and Corrupt Organizations Act, the Copyright Act, and the Jury Systems Improvement Act.[36] But such broad reading, although convenient to help reduce the federal courts' logjam of employment disputes,[37] is not necessarily borne out by the *Gilmer* decision, which is confined in application to the ADEA. Other statutes calling for a judicial remedy or trial by jury might yield different decisions.

Due Process Requirements

Aside from the due process issue of whether arbitration may reasonably be accepted before a dispute arises, the *Gilmer* decision recognizes the importance of due process components to any arbitration system for such system to be upheld by the courts. Although it found sufficient protections in the Stock Exchange arbitration system, a substantial doubt remains as to whether a fair system can be negotiated between a corporation and an individual employee, and whether the employer can be relied upon to establish a fair system to police its own activities. That issue of due process is bound to reappear until there is a widespread endorsement of what due process requirements an employer-promulgated system must include if it is to pass muster.

It is only natural for employers, or for those concerned with the well-being of employers, as in the security industry, to promulgate arbitration standards that are alleged to provide due process but that clearly serve employer interests. Such a report was issued by a security industry task force headed by SEC Chairman David Ruder in 1996. That report[38] recommended a cap of $750,000 or twice the actual damages (whichever is less), a reduction in the statute of limitations for arbitration claims from six to three years, selection of arbitrators from a longer list, earlier discovery, and raising the threshold to an undisclosed higher amount for which settlements must be reported beyond the current $5,000.

Summary

Increasing court concern for crowded dockets and delays, coupled with rising costs of litigation, appear to have led the Supreme Court and several circuit courts to a warm embrace of arbitration for resolution of statutory disputes. In revising its 1974 negative attitude toward arbitration into a glowing endorsement of the forum in its 1991 decision, the Court seems to have given a wider scope to arbitration of employment disputes than anticipated by the authors of the Federal Arbitration Act. It also seems to have glossed over a number of principles it had traditionally protected as "jealous mistress of the law." The courts since *Gilmer* have rushed to the same support of arbitration, while ignoring or indeed subverting multiple protections that had been the unique province of the judiciary.

While arbitration is a laudable and practical means for resolving numerous societal problems, the Supreme Court must provide the safeguards that will make arbitration as reliable a dispute settlement device as the courts. Due process protections of various types—in the scope of arbitration, the timing of the commitment to arbitrate, the qualification and selection of arbitrators, and the processing and hearing of the case itself—are necessary for the public, as well as the government agencies protecting public rights, to have faith in this substitute for the courts. Consistent with that good-faith reliance on the justice of such a system should be its right to provide the same type of remedies and damages as the courts, and the agencies' right to endorse awards to assure compliance with the laws of the land. Adoption of such due process protections remains a crucial item on the agenda of the Court as well as the nation.

Chapter Five

Employment Law Dispute Settlement Programs Developed by Private Business

The United States is one of the few industrialized countries adhering to the tradition of termination at will. Under that tradition the employment relationship is one voluntarily undertaken by the employee who opts to work for the enterprise. Management likewise voluntarily agrees to hire the employee to perform certain services for as long as both parties to that relationship wish it to continue. Either party is free to sever the relationship. Unlike many other countries, the United States does not provide a system of labor or industrial courts to determine the propriety of a termination action or to handle claims by employees that an employer's action violated the law. Employees may sue on the common law claims of breach of express or implied contract or on grounds of tort—but such litigation is relatively rare and costly to pursue—and should not be confused with the right to enforce statutory claims. As a result the termination at will doctrine remains largely immune from judicial interference.

Many people do not realize they have no governmental protection in the event of severance until their services are terminated. Some executive and professional contracts provide for arbitration to determine whether or not an employer's termination meets accepted standards of just cause, and all union contracts reached by collective bargaining do likewise. But for the more than 80 percent of the workforce employed in nonunion workplaces, there is no comparable neutral forum for ordinary workers to determine whether or not they were fired for just cause.

Some nonunion employers have sought to take a leaf from the book of the union sector by establishing procedures based on the collectively bargained grievance and arbitration model. These procedures seek to replicate that model by providing an employee a right of appeal to ever higher levels of management, culminating in a right of final appeal to an arbitrator selected by the employee from a list provided by the employer or perhaps even selected from the roster of a neutral agency such as the AAA. The motivation of the employer in providing such review may be to assure justice and fairness in the workplace. But the motivation may also be to forestall the rumbling of employee unrest that often flows from charges of unfair or arbitrary treatment of employees by supervisors and management, well known as the breeding ground for efforts at unionization. Perhaps such employers have hearkened to the adage that wayward employers rather than energetic unions are what generate labor organizations, and that the only employers under collective agreements are those that earn (or deserve) unionization. Regardless of the motivation, the evidence shows that over the years numerous nonunion employers have established grievance and arbitration systems for the resolution of disputes over discipline and discharge at the workplace.

There are some statutes that have provided employees protection against termination for seeking the enforcement of protected rights. Such legal rights extend to employees in both the union and nonunion sector. For example, the NLRA and the OSHA prohibit retaliatory action against employees who seek to avail themselves of the protections of the statutes. The governmental agency charged with enforcement of those statutes may initiate action against violating employers on behalf of complaining employees.

The passage of legislation prohibiting various forms of discrimination has also extended statutory protection against termination or other forms of adverse treatment to employees whose employers or their agents have violated the statutes. The prescribed relief for such statutory violations is usually through an administrative enforcement agency or through the courts.

The recent growth in employer-sponsored arbitration plans to resolve disputes over public law rights, while not universal, has become sufficiently widespread to constitute an important recourse for a significant number of employees. These numbers warrant examination as to the fairness of such procedures as an alternative to administrative and judicial review.

In 1995, the General Accounting Office issued a report on ADR methods based on a sample of two thousand businesses with more than one hundred employees and without collective bargaining coverage. Almost all the employers in the study used some form of ADR. Arbitration was one of the least common approaches, however, behind negotiations, fact-finding, mediation, and peer review. Only about 10 percent of employers used arbitration, and in only a minority of this group was arbitration mandatory for all covered employees. The General Accounting Office reported that it found some arbitration plans that did not meet the due process standards proposed by the Commission on the Future of Worker-Management Relations.[1]

This chapter is divided into two major sections. The first describes ten elements in a range of employer-designed arbitration plans, and the second discusses the role of the agencies that appoint arbitrators for employer-sponsored plans.

Elements of Employer-Designed Arbitration Plans

The Brown & Root Dispute Resolution Program,[2] effective 1993, is usually regarded as one of the most equitable employer-crafted structures for arbitrating statutory disputes in the aftermath of *Gilmer*. It consists of several efforts to resolve employment-related disputes prior to arbitration. Employees may choose to follow the sequence commencing with Option 1, Open Door Policy, to talk to an immediate supervisor or to any higher-level manager or to use a hot line to talk anonymously to an adviser in the Corporate Employee Relations Department. This option applies to "any concerns, questions or problems you may have with your supervisor or co-worker." The same range of problems is subject to Option 2, Conference, which involves meeting with a company representative and someone from the dispute resolution program to decide on the next course of action through the normal chain of command, through informal mediation by a Brown & Root mediator or an outside mediator or arbitrator. Outside mediation or arbitration constitute Options 3 and 4, selected in Option 2. For Option 3, the employee pays a $50 processing fee and the dispute is referred to the AAA, which arranges for the services of a professional mediator. Brown & Root pays any costs beyond the fee. The final Option 4 in the program is arbitration through the AAA of disputes involving legally protected rights such as protection against age, race, or sex discrimination, or sexual harassment. Again, the company pays any fees beyond the original $50 filing fee. The reference to outside arbitration can be used to resolve only those problems or disputes that "involve a legally protected right." Whether a dispute truly involves a legally protected right may also be determined at this time. The Legal Consultation Program provides for legal consultation with an attorney of the employee's choice. The Company pays 90 percent of the fee up to an annual benefit of $2,500 per employee in these cases.

Most employer-designed plans are introduced to employees with assurance that the goal is merely to reduce costs and delays of litigation while protecting the full rights of employees. The September 23, 1994, letter to site managers of AMS illustrates such an approach:

> AMS's policy has always been that all of our employees should be able to enjoy a work atmosphere free from any form of discrimination and harassment. Even aside from the legal risks our senior management finds all forms of discrimination and harassment unacceptable and inexcusable. However, we face a hard reality. Nationally, more and more charges are being filed with each passing year. The cost to defend any one charge is expensive. The cost to defend numerous charges can put a serious strain on our profitability. Every dollar we spend on legal fees is a dollar we cannot

reinvest in our business, our customers, employee training and development, compensation plans and other employee programs and service. Because we believe our hard earned profits are better spent being reinvested in our future, rather than being spent defending frivolous lawsuits, we are establishing a policy aimed at limiting the expense of defending employment related lawsuits.[3]

Condition of Employment

One of the most controversial issues in employment arbitration is the timing of the agreement to arbitrate. In union-management relations that agreement is made during the negotiation of the collective bargaining agreement. In commercial negotiations it is made during substantive negotiations to provide rapid and inexpensive recourse in the event of any dispute over the terms of that substantive agreement. Such negotiations are conducted knowingly by parties jointly willing to establish such procedures; the undertaking to arbitrate in such negotiations is almost incidental to the substantive agreement for the narrow purpose of expedited dispute resolution. But in the form of employment arbitration, which is the subject of the *Gilmer* decision, the arbitration is not mutually negotiated. Rather it is unilaterally developed by the employer. And it is usually not ancillary to a written contract of employment to rely on arbitration as the means of resolving disputes arising from that written employment agreement. Indeed, it is usually a separate contract or handbook for resolving a wide range of disputes—perhaps all disputes—with the employer without reference to the employment relationship, let alone the reasons for termination.

The *Gilmer* decision endorsed an arbitration agreement signed at the time of employment. This has signaled to employers that arbitration schemes agreed to by employees at the time of hire are acceptable to the courts. There has been a substantial increase in such arrangements that both existing and future employees are expected to sign. As noted in Chapter Four, current employees faced with the introduction of the new structure have little alternative but to sign if they expect to continue employment. The same pressure is present for job applicants. Critics claim that even the offering of such documents for signature when the program is newly introduced or at the time of hire makes them mandatory, and in effect, makes the signing a condition of continued or new employment. The other view is that such signings are voluntary, that employees are free to accept employment or reject it if such signing is a condition of continued employment or new hire, and to that extent the arbitration agreement is voluntary. A survey of some of the programs may help to resolve the issue of the extent to which such agreements are or are not mandatory conditions of continued employment or new hire.

The Brown & Root Dispute Resolution Program provides that its four-option plan is the exclusive means of resolving workplace disputes for legally protected rights. That means that if you accept or continue employment you will agree to resolve all legal claims against Brown & Root through its program instead of through governmental agencies and the courts. The resort to the first two steps of its options in cases that do not involve legally protected rights remains voluntary.

The ITT Corporation Headquarters Mediation and Arbitration Policy, effective February 1, 1994, reads in part as follows: "All Employees who continue employment after February 28, 1994 will be deemed to have accepted this policy as the exclusive method to resolve claims not resolved though informal procedures and, therefore, will not litigate claims in court or in judicial type proceedings before administrative agencies. . . . Any individual hired as an ITT Headquarters Employee after February 1, 1994 shall be deemed to have accepted this Policy."[4]

The Bridgestone/Firestone, Inc. Employee Dispute Resolution Plan[5] lists on its cover the following: "THE EMPLOYEE DISPUTE RESOLUTION PLAN BECOMES EFFECTIVE ON OCTOBER 1, 1995, AS THE EXCLUSIVE MEANS OF RESOLVING EMPLOYMENT-RELATED LEGAL CLAIMS. THAT MEANS

IF YOU APPLY FOR EMPLOYMENT, ACCEPT EMPLOY-
MENT, OR CONTINUE WORKING AT BRIDGESTONE/
FIRESTONE ON OR AFTER THAT DATE, YOU AGREE TO
RESOLVE ALL SUCH CLAIMS THROUGH THIS PROCESS,
INSTEAD OF THROUGH THE COURT SYSTEM OR
ADMINISTRATIVE AGENCIES."

On June 7, 1994, Bentley's Luggage Corporation sent a memorandum to all Bentley's Associates[6] citing the Company's "open
door" policy and noting: "By remaining a Bentley's employee, you
agree that, before filing any legal action regarding your employment
or the termination of your employment" it would be necessary to
follow the policy.

Some employers have offered carrots to those who sign up for
the programs. The AFM policy letter[7] contains the following:
"Please note that as a company policy, signing the agreement must
be a condition of continued employment with AFM. You'll note
the agreement also gives all employees a paid day off in consideration for signing and returning this agreement."

Other employers have offered sticks. In the covering letter
announcing the program to employees, Astra Personnel Manager
Roy W. Landgren noted:[8]

As you will remember, if you choose not to sign this agreement you
will not be eligible for future Profit Sharing allocations. The reason
for this is that in order for this agreement to be valid in many states,
a 'consideration' such as continued participation in the Astra Profit
Sharing Plan must be given in exchange for your signature. . . . I
wish to reemphasize that this is a totally voluntary program. Should
you choose not to sign the agreement it will be necessary for our
records that you sign the Form Declining Participation in the Arbitration Program so that proper future Profit Sharing allocations can
be made to eligible employees.

Employees of USWEST, Inc. receive notice of the obligation
to use arbitration for any disputes arising out of their employment

when they are issued a stock option grant in the US West Stock Option Program. The notice to employees encloses the Stock Option Schedule and a Stock Option Agreement containing the following arbitration commitment: "In consideration of the grant of the Option, the Optionee agrees that any dispute that may arise directly or indirectly in connection with the Plan, the Option, the Optionee's employment or the termination of the Optionee's employment, whether arising in contract, statute, tort, fraud, misrepresentation or other legal theory shall be determined solely by arbitration in Denver, Colorado, under the rules of the American Arbitration Association."[9]

Coverage of the Plan

In the union-management context, arbitration is invoked to resolve disputes arising under the terms of the collective bargaining agreement, including interpretation and application of the agreement as well as matters of discipline and discharge. In the nonunion sector, employers have the right to terminate at will, and there is seldom any written agreement calling for interpretation or application. Many employer-promulgated plans provide for an open-door discussion or even some form of mediation for a wide range of employee complaints. But the coverage changes at the arbitration step. The obvious intent of employer-promulgated arbitration plans is to invoke the use of arbitration to avoid the cost and delay of litigation (and in some cases to avoid the court's remedy) over matters that may arise before administrative agencies or the courts. That protection is sought in claims alleging the employer's statutory violations, which would otherwise be filed with the courts or administrative agencies. Such recourse is the expected appeal for claims of violation of various statutes involving discrimination, and most employer-promulgated arbitration schemes so specify. They also universally exclude arbitration of claims under workers' compensation and unemployment insurance laws. And most specify that they do not embrace a "just cause" standard for termination and do not alter the preexisting right of the employer to terminate at will (although one would assume that where the claim could show that the termination "at will" was itself a violation of the covered statutes, the statutes would control).

The notice covering the Bentley Agreement to Arbitrate contains the following common language: "The Company emphasizes and the employee hereby acknowledges that employment with Bentley's is at will and neither this application or any other document should be interpreted as creating a 'just cause' standard or contract of employment."[10]

An example of a broad coverage is illustrated by the ITT Headquarters Mediation and Arbitration Policy:[11]

> The Claims covered by this Policy include but are not limited to, claims for wages or other compensation due; claims for breach of any contract or covenant; tort claims; claims for discrimination including, but not limited to, race, color, sex, religion, national origin, disability, sexual orientation, marital status or age; claims for denial of benefits; claims for violation of any federal, state or other governmental law, statute, regulation or ordinance; and any other claims arising under common law. . . . The only claims not covered by this Policy are claims the Employee may have for workers compensation or unemployment compensation benefits.

The A.F.M. Services, Inc. (Archer) plan[12] requires claims alleging statutory violation to be filed with the appropriate federal, state, or local agency for an initial decision. However, the plan precludes appeal therefrom to the courts. If the employer prevails at the agency, the employee has a one-year period from the date of the agency decision to appeal to arbitration through the facilities of the AAA, "using a single arbitrator, which arbitrator shall be guided by applicable federal, state, and local discrimination and labor laws." The Archer plan would also require arbitration of "claims of any express or implied contract or tort claims." The plan also restricts the arbitrator from awarding punitive damages.[13]

The Hughes Aircraft Company[14] system requires as follows: "The Arbitrator shall interpret Company policy or rules and regulations and/or apply the substantive law (and the law of remedies, if applicable) of the state in which the claim arose, or federal law, or both, as applicable to the claim(s) asserted. The Federal Rules of Evidence shall apply. In reaching his or her decision the Arbitrator shall have no authority to change or modify any lawful Company policy, rule or regulation or the Arbitration Agreement."

Waiver of Right to Litigation

Most plans are explicit in citing the agreement being executed pursuant to the terms of the Federal Arbitration Act, and in noting that by signing up for arbitration, the claimant has waived any right to litigation. The Brown & Root Dispute Resolution Plan provides that if an employee files a lawsuit the Company "will ask the court to dismiss the case and refer it to our Dispute Resolution Program."[15] In the Archer Plan, even with its initial resort to the agency, any appeal is exclusively through arbitration without recourse to the courts. The agreement form for the plan so specifies, and even restricts challenges to that exclusion: "By you and Archer consenting to arbitrate claims as described above, this means that you and Archer are giving up your rights to bring such claims to court for trial and determination."[16] "Should any court determine that the agreement herein to submit to arbitration is not binding, or otherwise allows litigation, regarding claims covered herein, to proceed in a court of law, the parties hereto expressly waive any and all right to demand a jury in such litigation."[17]

Representation and Attorney's Fees

Most of the systems appear to grant charging employees the right to select their representative in the process, although the Hughes Aircraft Company Procedure[18] specifies that "no current or former supervisory or managerial employee of the Company shall represent another Employee."

The Travelers Group Employment Arbitration Policy[19] provides that "Any party may be represented by an attorney, a non-
supervisory co-worker or by him or her self. If an employee or
former employee chooses not to be represented by an attorney,
Travelers Group shall waive its right to be represented by an attorney unless such person is or was licensed to practice law in any
jurisdiction in the United States."

Most plans do not fund the cost of employee representation in
the procedure. Brown & Root offers to proceed without an attorney if the claimant does so, noting that "you may not have to share
an arbitrator's award with a lawyer," and is unique, as noted earlier,
in providing reimbursement of up to $2,500 for claimants' up-front
legal consultation, on approval of its program administrator.[20] ITT[21]
offers: "In the event arbitration results in an award greater than an
offer of settlement made by ITT to the Employee ITT will reim-
burse reasonable attorney's fees that the Employee incurred in
securing the arbitrator's award."

Arbitrator's Fees

There is great variation among the plans in their handling of the
cost of the neutral. Most programs call for sharing of the cost of the
arbitrator's fees and expenses between claimant and employer on a
fifty-fifty basis. The River Oaks Plan[22] calls for each party deposit-
ing its anticipated share of the arbitrator's fee in escrow, although
the "arbitrator may award reasonable fees to the prevailing party."
The Hughes EPRP Plan has a similar escrow provision but autho-
rizes the arbitrator on demonstration of an employee's "continuing
financial inability to pay his or her entire share of the Arbitrator's
fee" to order the company to "pay the employee's share of the fees
which exceed two weeks of wages."[23] The Brown & Root Program,
as noted earlier, calls for the employer to absorb all arbitration costs
above the employee's initial $50 filing fee. The Bridgestone/
Firestone Plan has a $100 threshold with the employer paying any
fees or expenses beyond that amount.[24] In the ITT Plan the

employer pays 90 percent of the cost of mediation and 75 percent of the cost of arbitration, including in both percentages, the administrative fees of the AAA and the fees and expenses of the neutral.[25]

Under the Traveler's Employment Arbitration Policy,[26] the employer picks up the cost of the arbitrator for employees earning $150,000 or less. It does require payment of a $50 administration fee and sharing of costs beyond one day of hearing, a requirement that may not be disturbed by the arbitrator's award.

Administering Agency

Most plans appear to use either the AAA or J.A.M.S./Endispute. Those invoking the AAA in the past have varied in applying its commercial rules, its employment rules, or its labor arbitration rules. Those alternatives have now been replaced by the requirement that employment cases must use the new *National Rules for the Resolution of Employment Disputes*. The Hughes system lists both agencies as providers, but the party that did not initiate the claim has the option of selecting which agency shall administer the arbitration.[27] The selection of the arbitrator is usually by alternate striking of names from a list provided by the agency or by preference listing with the agency to designate the highest mutual choice.

Statute of Limitations

In most procedures, the time for filing claims is shorter than the statutes of limitations applicable under the various discrimination laws. Astra USA, Inc. calls for written notice demanding arbitration and setting forth the specific nature of the claim "to the Company not later than 180 days after the date the employee learned or should have learned of the facts forming the basis of the claim(s)."[28] The Hughes Aircraft Company's EPRP Arbitration Procedure provides for a formal notice of intent to arbitrate following completion of the internal claim review by the EPRP Consensus Review Board:[29] "Employees must give written notice to the HAC of any claim to be arbitrated. An Employee must give notice of any claim within twenty (20) working days of the decision date of the EPRP Consensus Review Board, and within any applicable federal or state statute of limitations."

The Bridgestone/Firestone Plan[30] establishes a deadline for appeal to arbitration "within thirty (30) days from date that the Mediation process has been concluded. Failure of a Party to timely initiate a proceeding hereunder shall bar the Party from any relief or other proceedings under this Plan or otherwise, and any such dispute shall be deemed to have been finally and completely resolved."

Discovery

Many advocates of arbitration cite the cost and delays of discovery as one of the justifications for avoiding litigation. Under the *Protocol*, reasonable resort to deposition and discovery is permitted with supervision and discretion over the procedures residing in the hands of the arbitrator. But one notices a tendency in employer-created programs to severely restrict such access to information. The A.F.M. Archer program[31] agreement restricts the arbitrator as follows: "The parties agree that in any arbitration the Arbitrator shall be limited to allowing parties pre-hearing discovery at least ten (10) days prior to the scheduled arbitration date, which shall consist only of there being a mutual exchange of lists containing the names of witnesses, including expert witnesses to be used and a copy of all proposed exhibits to be used."

In the River Oaks Mutual Agreement to Arbitrate Claims, the discovery provision[32] reads as follows: "Each party shall have the right to take the deposition of one individual and any expert witness designated by another party. Each party will also have the right to make requests for production of documents to any party. . . . Additional discovery may be had only where the Arbitrator selected pursuant to this Agreement so orders, upon a showing of substantial need."

Duration

Since the procedures are unilaterally promulgated, most reserve to the employer the sole discretion over the cancellation of the programs. The language of the ITT program[33] is typical in this regard: "ITT reserves the right to change or discontinue this Policy at any time upon prior written notice to Employees from the ITT Headquarters Human Resources Department except that any claim submitted under this Policy to mediation or arbitration before the effective date of any modification or discontinuance shall continue to be resolved through this Policy as it existed before modification or discontinuance."

Arbitrator's Award

Most policies call for a fully written opinion and award, some specifying that the award be issued within thirty days of the hearing and others providing additional time. Some provide for submission of post-hearing briefs by the parties' representatives. But the policies vary on the arbitrator's authority on the subject of remedy, though several permit award of costs. Brown & Root provides among the most liberal policies, specifying that the arbitrator "has the same authority as a judge in making awards to employees."[34] The AFM policy[35] restricts the arbitrator and any reviewing court by noting: "Should the arbitrator's decision find in favor of the employee, the employee waives his/her right to receive punitive damages. Employees still have the right to be awarded job reinstatement, back pay, and compensatory damages, where appropriate.

"Should a court rule this agreement is not binding, litigation in court will be heard by a judge, rather than a jury, and punitive damages will not be a part of the remedies available to aggrieved parties."

The Bentley program[36] specifies: "In any arbitration involving a legal claim, the arbitrator shall interpret the relevant common law or statutory provisions, and may award all compensatory damages that would be available from a court. In no case will punitive damages be available." A similar scope of relief is anticipated by the Travelers Group Program:[37]

> The arbitrator shall have the power to award, in appropriate circumstances, money damages in an amount sufficient to compensate the aggrieved party for such direct injury as the arbitrator determines such party has suffered. The arbitrator shall have the authority to order reinstatement of employment of a former employee only if money damages are insufficient as a remedy. Unless expressly provided for by the applicable statute, the arbitrator shall not have the authority to award punitive damages, attorney's fees or injunctive relief of any nature. The arbitrator shall not have the authority to make any award that is arbitrary or capricious, or to award to Travelers Group the costs of the arbitration that it is otherwise required to bear under this policy.

The Astra Program[38] is more specific on remedy authority of the arbitrator:

> The arbitrator may make one or more of the following awards if the finding is for the employee:
>
> 1. reinstatement to the position of employment the employee held or if that is impractical, to a comparable position.
>
> 2. full or partial back pay and reimbursement for lost fringe benefits, without interest, reduced by interim earnings, benefits received, and amounts that could have been received with reasonable diligence.
>
> 3. if reinstatement is not practical or reasonable under the circumstances, but is nevertheless warranted, the arbitrator may award up to 12 months of front pay.
>
> 4. the arbitrator may award punitive damages up to 12 months pay.

The Primerica Dispute Resolution Program[39] prescribes: "The arbitrator shall have the power to award, in circumstances, money damages in an amount sufficient to compensate the aggrieved party for such direct injury as the arbitrator determines such party has suffered. The arbitrator shall have the authority to order reinstatement of employment to an employee only if money damages are insufficient as a remedy. The arbitrator shall not have the authority to award punitive damages to either party, or to award to Primerica the costs of the grievance procedure or arbitration that it is otherwise required to bear under this policy."

Judicial Review

As noted throughout this chapter, the sponsors of these programs anticipate the endorsement of the arbitration agreement by the courts as providing a final and binding resolution of the dispute. There is usually provision for appeal to a court for enforcement. Indeed, in the arbitration agreement, it is not uncommon to see a penalty imposed on the party seeking to overturn the arbitration award. As noted in the USWEST, Inc. Stock Options Agreement:[40]

> The decision of the arbitrator (i) shall be final and binding, (ii) shall be rendered within 90 days after the impanelment of the arbitrator, and (iii) shall be kept confidential by the parties to such arbitration. The arbitration award may be enforced by any court of competent jurisdiction. The Federal Arbitration Act and not state law shall govern the arbitrability of all claims.
>
> If any party hereto files a judicial or administrative action asserting claims subject to this arbitration provision and another party successfully stays such actions and/or compels arbitration of such claims, the party filing said action shall pay the other party's costs and expenses incurred in seeking such stay and/or compelling arbitration, including reasonable attorney's fees.

Role of the Designating Agencies

Many of the employer-promulgated systems have used the services of the AAA or other agencies to administer their programs. Traditionally, the AAA followed the policy of administering the arbitration program as presented to it. It established and maintained separate rules for the conduct of the various types of arbitrations it administered. It had different rules for labor-management disputes, commercial disputes, construction disputes, and so on. Whether an arbitrator was bound by the agreement to arbitrate or the rules of the designating agency depended upon whether the arbitration agreement controlled or whether the parties to that arbitration agreement had agreed to have the arbitration administered pursuant to the agency rules. The arbitrator drew authority from the parties' agreement, and if that agreement contained any of the restrictions discussed earlier in this chapter, the arbitrator was bound by those rules unless the agreement contained a clause deferring to the rules of the designating agency.

Since the establishment of the *Protocol*, both the AAA and J.A.M.S./Endispute have reexamined their policies to assure that the employer-promulgated systems they administer do provide the type of fairness historically expected from arbitration agreements between two corporations in commercial arbitration or between unions and management under collective bargaining agreements. That reexamination led to a revision of prior rules first by J.A.M.S./Endispute and several months later by the AAA, whose *National Rules for the Resolution of Employment Disputes* went into effect on June 1, 1996. Under their current policies, both organizations will continue to administer employer-promulgated arbitration agreements even if initiated at the time of hire or introduced as a condition of continuing employment. But both organizations have included in their rules the requirement that they administer cases only in conformity with the standards of the *Protocol*. The new rules of both designating agencies reflect this policy.

As a consequence, many employers whose systems use the services of J.A.M.S./Endispute or the AAA will discover that old restrictive practices will have to give way to *Protocol* standards. For example, Section 1 of the AAA's *National Rules for the Resolution of Employment Disputes* now provides as follows: "The Parties shall be deemed to have made these rules a part of their arbitration agreement whenever they have provided for Arbitration by the AAA, or under its *National Rules for the Resolution of Employment Disputes*. If a party establishes that a material inconsistency exists between the arbitration agreement and these rules the arbitrator shall apply these rules."[41]

Arbitrators whose prior allegiance was to the parties' arbitration agreement are now to be governed by the due process rules of the designating agencies. Under the AAA rules requiring adherence thereto, it is left to the arbitrator to resolve conflicts between the agreement and the AAA rules in favor of the AAA rules. As of January 1, 1997, the AAA no longer allows use of its own commercial or labor-management rules in employment disputes. Instead, it administers "all employment cases arising out of employer-promulgated ADR programs under the *National Rules for the Resolution of Employment Disputes*, even if the arbitration clause or dispute resolution program calls for a different set of rules."

Summary

Although some employers have for years imposed arbitration agreements on their new or existing employees, such schemes raised wider issues in 1991 when the *Gilmer* decision made such arbitration agreements enforceable in the courts. Numerous employers thereafter have sought benefit from the courts' endorsement of their unilaterally imposed systems. As a review of ten elements of employer-promulgated plans has demonstrated, there are very wide differences in the due process quality of these plans.

A few systems, such as Brown & Root, have sought to provide the full range of legal protections and remedies through a cheaper and speedier resort to arbitration, albeit as a condition of employment. Others have merely sought to secure the perception of fairness by inserting in the rules that they were to be administered by neutral designating agencies, even though the administration would be pursuant to the terms of the prescribed arbitration agreement. An issue that arises, however, with virtually all employer-promulgated plans is the reservation to the employer of the sole right to modify or to terminate the plan.

In 1996, with the integration of the *Protocol* into the rules of J.A.M.S./Endispute and the AAA, employers seeking the protective umbrella of such agencies must expect to have their systems administered pursuant to rules of fair play as reflected in the new agency rules. Whether this change will lead employers to find more compliant administrators or lead to more due process administration remains to be seen. There are some indications at this early date that due process procedures may be gaining in employer-promulgated plans.[42]

Chapter Six

Elements of Due
Process Protection

Assuring due process protection is probably the most crucial issue in establishing a private dispute resolution system in employment law disputes. It is essential if such a system is to substitute for recourse to administrative agencies and the courts.

Society has come to accept the existing machinery administered by government agencies, subject to the final review of the courts, as the accepted standard of fairness. That fairness is manifest in the procedural protections accorded by the agencies and monitored by the courts, which may reverse or remand when the agency is found to have violated accepted standards of due process. The judicial model is thus the benchmark against which to examine any dispute settlement machinery asserted to be its reasonable substitute.

The courts have often been described as the jealous mistress of the law,[1] unwilling to share their final authority with any institution perceived as lacking their societal mandate to bring finality to disputes. That distrust extended to arbitrators. The NLRB, faced with the authority of arbitrators to render final and binding interpretations of collective bargaining agreements, recognized a potential conflict with its statutory responsibility by developing its standards of arbitral deferral. It developed a standard for reviewing the arbitrator's decision in areas of joint jurisdiction. The NLRB's current standard as reflected in the *Spielberg-Olin* decisions defers to the arbitrators, rejecting only those decisions it finds repugnant to its reading of the statute. The reasoning of the Supreme Court has followed a similar path. As noted in the Chapter Four discussion of *Alexander* v. *Gardner-Denver,* the Court declared its willingness to permit arbitrators to make findings of fact, while reserving to the courts the authority to interpret and apply the law—including questions of due process protections. That decision is still the law of the land on arbitration of collective bargaining agreements, and governs the union-management community entrusted by the *Steelworkers Trilogy* with protecting the sanctity of its own industrial jurisprudence.

The advent of *Gilmer* in 1991, with its full endorsement of arbitration agreements, constitutes a change in the Court's jealous mistress position, at least in the employment discrimination field. That decision also constituted a surrender of the Court's procedural authority to require due process in the application of the statutes under its suzerainty. If such procedures are to be insulated by *Gilmer* from review or interference by the courts, then the creators of private machinery need not worry about the Court's review of the fairness of their processes. In the current debate over alternative dispute machinery, the *Gilmer* approach is that such external machinery is endorsed because the parties voluntarily subscribed to it. That view suggests that the parties to such arbitration agreements, even if disparate in power, voluntarily struck a deal with which the court will not tamper.

On the other hand, if *Gilmer*-endorsed arbitration remains so unapproachable on the issue of statutory finality, it remains incumbent on the courts to exercise the right to review the propriety of such machinery or its results. This is a vital constraint on the developers of such processes to assure that their procedures are fair and just. In developing such alternative machinery, the role of the courts should be to assure citizens that their due process rights are protected when substantive decision making moves from the courts to private dispute resolvers, and that arbitration is only a substitution of forum and not a denial of statutory rights.

Regardless of whether employers are permitted unfettered control over their internal arbitration structures, or whether the courts assert that role to assure protection of due process under such schemes, credibility requires that such systems should be fair and should include due process protections. That simply makes good business sense. Otherwise these systems will have little standing with employees, with the organizations asserting claimant rights, with the press, or with the community at large—let alone with the courts.

This chapter examines under eleven headings what we believe to be the essential standards of due process that any system must embrace if it is to replicate the judicial protections society requires. These headings encompass and elaborate on the standards of the *Protocol*. (See Appendix B for the full text.) It is assumed that mediation will be available as a preliminary and preferred process for resolving each dispute.

Voluntarism

Probably the most contentious issue in statutory arbitration is whether or not employment arbitration agreements are mandatory or voluntary. In the union-management model, unions and managements jointly and voluntarily negotiate a procedure making arbitration the prescribed means to resolve interest disputes or prospective rights disputes during the term of their collective agreement. Arbitrators are usually given the responsibility to determine the range of contractual protections. For any individual employee who is covered by the collectively negotiated agreement, including those who later come to work in that enterprise under the terms of that agreement, arbitration is indeed mandatory. Arbitration becomes the sole venue for resolving disputes under that agreement. But in that employment context, the mandate to arbitrate extends only within the four corners of the agreement. The employee—though bound to use arbitration for resolving disputes under that agreement—still has the right to file a claim or bring suit for alleged violations of employment law.

A different situation occurs with arbitration agreements outside the union environment. In the nonunion workplace, except perhaps for executives and managers, there is no negotiation of the arbitration procedure with the employee, let alone with a union or with a committee of workers. The employer alone develops the arbitration procedure, and understandably inserts elements that favor its position. It establishes a system that is the same for all its employees, without individual employee option for procedural change. Aside from some executives and high-powered professional employees, no individual—even if given the opportunity to share in the development of such a system—can reasonably be expected to match the negotiating power of the enterprise.

Therefore, the issue of voluntarism arises over whether rank-and-file job applicants or employees faced with a choice of signing the arbitration agreement or losing their jobs have any option. May they decline to be bound without any adverse consequences? Will they still get the jobs for which they came? Will they keep the jobs they long occupied before the employer introduced the arbitration scheme?

The motivation of the employer in developing an arbitration system is to require employees to use that system instead of litigation to resolve employment disputes. In that process the enterprise will save substantial litigation costs. It can further benefit by establishing favorable terms for itself with an arbitration structure that bars punitive damages or imposes a cap on the arbitrator's remedy authority and avoids the risk of potentially costly jury awards. That is most effectively accomplished by securing employee commitment to arbitrate before any dispute arises, and before the employee has a specific issue over which to weigh the alternatives of arbitration or litigation.

To accomplish that objective employers most often provide the arbitration alternative to employees at the time of initial employment. It may be offered as a form to sign when being hired; it may be explained in detail before being asked to sign; or it may be offered as an alternative after the decision to hire is announced. Clearly, once the arbitration agreement is signed, arbitration becomes mandatory. The issue is whether the signing should be mandatory as a condition of hire or continued employment. Is it a specified or implied condition of employment, or is the individual free to decline without fear of retaliation? That is the nub of the "voluntary" issue. Many employers claim that partaking in such preexisting systems is a condition of employment. They argue that employees who wish to work for that enterprise voluntarily subscribe to such a condition just as they conform to many other conditions of employment, since they are free to decline the job offer.

Many employee advocates take the position that such agreements to arbitrate are not voluntary if an applicant's employment depends upon them. They argue that job applicants are in effect coerced into signing at the risk of being refused needed work. They assert that if someone is required to sign the arbitration agreement prior to an actual dispute, without knowledge of the impact of the signature on a particular statutory claim and without any viable alternatives, that such an advance commitment to arbitrate can hardly be termed voluntary.

The same reasoning would apply to a plan newly introduced by the employer for its existing workforce. Are those currently employed free to decline to subscribe to the plan without fear of termination or retaliation over assignments, raises, promotions, or other conditions of employment?

Despite the argument that any request to commit to arbitration constitutes coercion, either at the time of hire or when a new system is introduced, it is possible to posit a fairer system. That would occur where declining to sign brings no adverse consequences, where the employee would still be hired, would still get the promotion or raise, and would not be otherwise retaliated against for the refusal. Employees effectively exercising the option of not signing up for arbitration might have recourse to litigation if the employer's failure to provide the same benefits as to signing employees constituted a violation of some discrimination statute. But such a course could be hazardous.

The postdispute agreement to arbitrate is obviously immune from challenge on grounds of coercion. At that point the option of whether or not to use arbitration is made with full knowledge of the other alternatives. Arbitration chosen by both parties at that point is obviously voluntary. However, the alternative of litigation being readily available may preclude joint agreement to arbitrate if either party believes it has a stronger case, and acceptable risks, by proceeding to court. Permitting the election for arbitration to be made after the dispute has arisen reduces the likelihood of resort to arbitration compared to when the commitment is made predispute.

As noted in Chapter Four, the Commission on the Future of Worker-Management Relations, the Secretary of Labor's Task Force on Excellence in State and Local Government Through Union-Management Cooperation, and those government agencies that have embraced arbitration of statutory disputes propose that the agreement to arbitrate be postdispute. They espouse the view that an agency might not be willing to permit arbitration of all statutory disputes arising in the employment context. That would be particularly so when the dispute involves criminal or class actions or landmark issues that the agency may wish to litigate so as to establish an important precedent for future cases. Only when the statutory claim arises can one make an intelligent assessment of whether litigation or arbitration is more desirable, and if arbitration is preferred, whether the system offered provides the requisite protections to assure a fair hearing and decision.

The Due Process Task Force, unable to reach agreement on the triggering event for initiation of its recommended procedures, stated in the introduction to the *Protocol*: "The Task Force takes no position on the timing of agreements to mediate and/or arbitrate statutory employment disputes, though it agrees that such agreements be knowingly made. The focus of this protocol is on standards of exemplary due process."

The AAA's 1997 *National Rules for Resolution of Employment Disputes* provide that even if the employee has agreed to mandatory arbitration as a condition of employment, the AAA will only administer cases that conform to its rules, holding off for sixty days to permit court challenge as to whether the agreement to arbitrate was voluntarily and knowingly signed. As of January 1, 1997 (as noted at the end of Chapter Five), the AAA required all employment cases arising out of employer-promulgated ADR programs to be administered under its revised national rules for employment disputes, regardless of the rules specified in the employer's program. J.A.M.S./Endispute has also endorsed the *Protocol* and redesigned the rules to achieve its implementation.[2]

Scope of the Arbitration

Employer-promulgated arbitration systems generally contemplate that *all* employee disputes with the employer be submitted to arbitration under the employer's scheme. That procedure contrasts to those negotiated under collective bargaining agreements, which specify the issues to be arbitrated and the standards for contract interpretation. In the absence of collective bargaining, the employer has the unilateral discretion to determine what matters are to be the subject of the arbitration procedure. Many employers' plans offer arbitration over issues of company adherence to its own rules, and even to the propriety of discipline and discharge. To the extent that such an employer is willing to subject any of its actions to external review, it may be argued that the employer provides greater employee protection than would be provided in working for an employer without such machinery.

But the coverage that is most in dispute under employer-promulgated plans is the arbitration of claims of statutory violation. It is under this coverage that employees forfeit their right to file administrative claims or initiate litigation against their employer for breaking the law. Here the employer is usually seeking not merely to avoid the consequences of a jury verdict, or delayed court resolution, or having to pay court costs, attorney fees, and damages.

It is placing limitations on the scope of arbitration, to put beyond the arbitrator's authority the right to impose punitive damages that might be ordered in a court of law.

Representation

Unlike the union-management model, where the union provides automatic representation of the claimant at the several steps of the grievance and arbitration system, there is usually no comparable right of free representation for the employee in the employer-promulgated system. In a few cases, the employer provides some funding. The employee may be alone in challenging the employer in the employer-promulgated system, with no entitlement to representation. In some of the more draconian systems, employees are required to proceed on their own, without the right to hire external representation. Such provisions often come with the pious exhortation, "We want to keep our disputes within the family." In most cases, employers permit employees to have representation, but the cost is borne by the individual claimant. In a few cases, the employer provides some subsidy for representation. Brown & Root bears 90 percent of the cost of employee legal representation up to a cap of $2,500 per year per employee.[3] One would think that the plaintiff bar, operating on a contingency fee arrangement, might provide an adequate network of legal assistance in pursuing such claims. As it turns out, however, the need to provide a substantial initial retainer to hire such an attorney effectively restricts access to such representation—especially when one considers that 60 percent of the families in the workforce, many with two wage earners, earn less than $35,000 per year. Experience to date shows that employees in professional and executive ranks are most likely to use these systems and, indeed, even the public law procedures. But the prospect of expanded coverage to all employees, including the lower-paid, makes provision of representation a matter of growing concern. Even the prospect of securing reimbursement of legal fees in an arbitrator's award is rarely enough to lure the plaintiff bar to represent lower-paid wage earners—and such reimbursement, if provided at all, normally occurs only when the employee wins, not if he or she loses.

Nonetheless, due process in arbitration requires that an employee be assured access to representation as easily as in litigation, that the employee have the option of determining whether representation be by lawyer or layperson, and that the selection of that representative be left exclusively to the employee. Professional competence is necessary to provide representation comparable to that most certainly retained by the employer. Statutory knowledge and professional expertise is requisite to prepare and handle depositions and discovery, to share in the selection of the arbitrator, to examine and cross-examine witnesses during the hearing, and to prepare and present the closing arguments or brief. The funding of such representation remains a serious problem in attempting to assure due process. Most wage earners cannot afford attorneys for long-lasting litigation, but since a much more rapid process is involved in arbitration than litigation (and the former also avoids costly appeals), the outlay for legal representation in arbitration should be substantially less.

Representational assistance is vital for employees in confronting statutory issues, particularly when the employer is represented by counsel well versed in the statutory issues in dispute. In judicial proceedings, the courts frequently make provision for counsel to assist claimants. Arbitrators may not have the authority to provide such representation but they must assure that the proceedings are fair and that claimants acting pro se, or represented by counsel unfamiliar with the statutory issues, still encounter a fair process. When aware that the employer is taking untoward advantage of the claimant's lack of adequate representation, the arbitrator should not serve as counsel for the under- or unrepresented claimant, but should urge the claimant to seek qualified counsel or guidance. This underscores the need for arbitrators to know the statutes and pertinent case law. The possible imbalance in qualified representation demonstrates the importance of such assistance by legal assistance organizations, civil rights groups, or labor organizations. For unions in particular, this representation role opens the door to fertile organizing activity.

The *Protocol*, like the AAA *National Rules for Resolution of Employment Disputes,* provides that the agency designating the arbitrator will also make suggestions to the claimant for representation. The Massachusetts Commission Against Discrimination (MCAD) is committed to providing staff representation to claimants who would otherwise proceed on their own. Such support is provided in litigation for cases that come to it directly. Because arbitration is substantially less expensive and less time-consuming than court proceedings, the Commission believes that the practice saves resources it would otherwise spend to represent employees through often tortuous litigation and appeals.

The *Protocol* sets forth the following standards on the right of representation: "B1. Choice of Representative. Employees considering the use of or, in fact, utilizing mediation and/or arbitration procedures should have the right to be represented by a spokesperson of their own choosing. The mediation and arbitration procedure should so specify and should include reference to institutions which might offer assistance, such as bar associations, legal service associations, civil rights organizations, trade unions, etc."

Arbitrator Qualifications

Arbitration presumes the mutual selection of an individual authorized by the parties to resolve their dispute. It is assumed that the arbitrator is knowledgeable in the subject matter of the dispute and has no prehearing bias in favor of either party to the arbitration.

Arbitrator neutrality is established by more than joint selection by the disputing parties. Neutrality is the independence to decide a case as readily for one side as for the other. In the union-management arena, neutrality is recognized and assumed in the cadre of the several hundred individuals who arbitrate the great majority of the grievances. They are known to the parties from distribution or publication of prior decisions and from their reputation among

practitioners for fairness in the conduct of the hearing and in decisions. Their reputations for integrity and independence help them
survive in a competitive market where thousands are available for
the work. They are expected to follow a Code of Professional
Responsibility for Arbitrators of Labor-Management Disputes. The
most seasoned and most acceptable have achieved their status
by "calling 'em as they see 'em." Those who fail to achieve that status may be prone to split decisions or decide cases with a prime
commitment to maintaining their acceptability. The parties usually recognize the strength or weakness of their case and it is sur-
prise more than loss that will lead to doubts of the arbitrator's future
suitability.

Union-management arbitrator qualification also presupposes
knowledge of the substantive matters in dispute. In the early days
of collective bargaining, arbitration neutrals gained their substantive knowledge from prior representation of the parties and from
teaching classes in industrial and labor relations and labor law.
With the advent of public sector collective bargaining and the
spread of arbitration into jurisdictions lacking the traditional industrial base, new neutrals came into the field with less background in
traditional industrial relations. They have nonetheless earned
acceptability for their fairness and impartiality, moving into private
sector work, as well.

Different pressures are confronted in the new field of statutory
arbitration, making the union-management standards of neutrality
and substantive expertise quite distinguishable. In the ADR field,
the arbitrator's responsibility is quite different from protection of
the parties' relationship and the interpretation and application of
the parties' private negotiated collective bargaining agreement. It
runs to a much more public purpose, that is, applying statutory
standards and regulations to private disputes. Union-management
arbitrators, even those who are lawyers, seldom feel the need to
be current in discrimination law, regulations, statutes, or court
decisions. Confinement to the four corners of the collective bargaining agreement—along with the presence of qualified representation on both sides—has usually made such legal expertise

relatively unnecessary. Despite their qualifications in the conduct of collective-bargaining arbitration proceedings, lack of substantive knowledge of the case law and the statutes being invoked by the claimants may make union-management arbitrators unacceptable for employment law dispute resolution or uninterested in it—or even intimidated by it.

Certainly there are union-management arbitrators with knowledge and experience in employment law. But the arbitrators of statutory issues, more likely, will be those with statutory and legal expertise and experience gained as litigators and advocates. But distinguishable from the union-management field, the "right" decision is more likely to be a product reflecting the state of the law, a subject a fair-minded advocate would be able to rule on despite prior professional employment by one side or the other. In a sense, this is not unlike the genesis of the collective-bargaining arbitration profession. In an earlier era, before the cadre of full-time arbitrators emerged, it was not uncommon for the parties to select as their arbitrator a respected person who had in fact served as a representative of one of the parties. To this day the Arbitrators Code of Professional Responsibility permits senior arbitrators who are "grandfathered" to serve as advocates as well as arbitrators, provided they do not present cases before fellow members of the National Academy of Arbitrators (NAA). As in collective-bargaining arbitration, the role of the employment law arbitrator should be open to lawyer and nonlawyer alike. Just as nonlawyers rose to the pinnacles of acceptability and competence in collective-bargaining arbitration, so too should they in statutory arbitration. In any event, the parties should have the freedom to select the neutral they want without being restricted by arbitrary standards of legal certification.

In the present infancy of statutory arbitration, we are going through the same procedure. The parties select an arbitrator they deem the most qualified and knowledgeable of the law, despite that individual's prior or ongoing role as an arbitrator of union-management disputes or as an advocate for other parties. Thus in the ADR field the term *neutral* takes on a new meaning. While it still requires the arbitrator to be as willing to decide for one side as the other, that neutrality is required only for the individual case. At present the parties do not expect the arbitrator to maintain the full-time or regular neutral practice that may characterize this type of work in the future. In the initial employment panel of the MCAD, of some thirty arbitrators approximately a quarter were identified as union-management arbitrators. The majority were advocates.

Section C1 of the *Protocol* provides in part: "Regardless of their prior experience, mediators and arbitrators on the roster must be independent and free of bias toward either party. They should reject cases if they believe the procedure lacks requisite due process."

The term *due process* therefore raises different expectations in the statutory field than it does in the labor relations field. Certainly independence of judgment and integrity are required in both arenas. Substantive expertise in union-management relations must give way to legal expertise in applying the statutes and court decisions in a manner that will ensure a fair hearing, with adequate representation for the participants. That will induce acceptance of the arbitrator's awards by the agencies and courts, and hopefully by the parties as well in their future use of the procedures. Proponents of statutory arbitration are obliged to assure that the new cadre of arbitrators is qualified to take on the role that has heretofore been the province of the agencies and the courts.

The *Protocol* in Section C1 anticipates the following qualifications: "Mediators and arbitrators selected for such cases should have skill in the conduct of hearings, knowledge of the statutory issues at stake in the dispute and familiarity with the workplace and employment environment."

Arbitrator Training

Attainment of that requisite expertise will require introductory and ongoing training. Union-management arbitrators who are acceptable to the parties in statutory cases have a long tradition of moving into different work environments with different employment relationships, and of course with different issues. They have had the luxury of representation by both parties, which can quickly educate them to the specifics of the issues in dispute. They do not have that luxury of relying on equally adept representatives when handling statutory issues. There will be need to train them in the statutes and the rules and regulations of the agencies and the holdings of the courts. There will also be need for training traditional union-management arbitrators in procedural issues that may be new to them such as depositions and discovery, and in the intricacies of damages, fee allocation, and punitive damages. For those with experience and backgrounds as litigators there is need for training in the procedures and techniques of mediation and arbitration and the conduct of hearings. They also need to become acquainted with the professional responsibilities of a neutral, the decision-making process, the writing of opinions, and the like. Arbitrator résumés should list courses, including the statutes studied, to enlighten potential selectors of the arbitrator as to the relative expertise possessed for the issues to be arbitrated.

To facilitate arbitrator training, the AAA in cooperation with the ABA undertook a series of local training programs for its new Employment Panel beginning in October 1996. The first year is dedicated to procedural training in discovery, remedies, ethical issues, and depositions, in addition to a wide variety of procedural problems faced during a hearing. The second round of training embraces matters of substantive concern, such as the various discrimination statutes.

Section C1 of the *Protocol* calls for training to be provided by those familiar with the conduct of arbitration hearings and those familiar with the state of the various laws under scrutiny.

1. Roster Membership . . .

The existing cadre of labor and employment mediators and arbitrators, some lawyers, some not, although skilled in conducting hearings and familiar with the employment milieu is unlikely without special training to consistently possess knowledge of the statutory environment in which these disputes arise and of the characteristics of the non-union workplace.

There is manifest need for mediators and arbitrators with expertise in statutory requirements in the employment field, who may, without special training, lack experience in the employment area, and in the conduct of arbitration hearings and mediation sessions. . . .

2. Training

There is manifest need for mediators and arbitrators with expertise in statutory requirements in the employment field, who may, without special training, lack experience in the employment area, and in the conduct of arbitration hearings and mediation sessions. . . . Training in the statutory issues should be provided by the government agencies, bar associations, academic institutions, etc. administered perhaps by the designating agency, such as the AAA, at various locations throughout the country. Such training should be updated periodically and be required of all mediators and arbitrators. Training in the conduct of mediation and arbitration could be provided by a mentoring program with experienced panelists.

Arbitrator Diversity

Due process in the selection of arbitrators requires that they come from a pool in which the claimants have confidence. With a workforce nearly half female and with many claimants in discrimination issues coming from minorities, the pool needs to be one that is perceived as potentially fair and representative of the workforce—and thus demographically diverse. The current pool of union-management arbitrators is not diverse. Whether it reflects a white male-dominated workforce or a white male-dominated group of arbitrator selectors on the union and management sides, the fact remains that only 10 percent of the membership of the NAA is female; an even smaller percentage is black or Hispanic. The nonunion workforce tends to be diversified and is entitled to have access to females and minorities as arbitrators of their statutory disputes, particularly those arising from claims of discrimination. Even if all the NAA members undertook to do this work, however, there are too few female and minority arbitrators to meet the needs of the total workforce. Indeed, even if all the arbitrators on the AAA or the FMCS panels were to add these cases to their present workload, there is no likelihood that, even if acceptable, they could fulfill the anticipated demand. The designating agencies putting together the arbitration panels from which selections are to be made for individual cases are obliged to expand the roster of females and minorities substantially to create credibility of the system. Greater demographic diversity in the roster, when viewed in the context of the predominantly white male composition of the courts, may encourage greater use of the private facilities in hope of greater and more acceptable justice. The *Protocol* provides in Section C1: "The roster of available mediators and arbitrators should be established on a non-discriminatory basis, diverse by gender, ethnicity, background, experience, etc. to satisfy the parties that their interest and objectives will be respected and fully considered."

Arbitrator Selection

In the union-management arena, the designation of arbitrators is handled by the parties agreeing on a selection procedure. That includes agreeing on a permanent single arbitrator, a panel of arbitrators, or an arbitrator for a pending case. In the absence of agreement, it means invoking the procedures of an established designating agency such as the AAA or the FMCS, which typically submits a list of names. If those names are rejected, the agency may appoint the arbitrator. The parties know—or find out from the grapevine—about the practices, biases, and philosophy of the acceptable arbitrators. If an unknown name appears on the list of a designating agency it is unlikely that the parties will immediately agree to use that person, opting instead for arbitrators whose track record they have long had under scrutiny. New arbitrators often have a particularly difficult time securing the caseload needed to create a track record.

In the statutory area, however, scrutiny of the arbitrators cannot be as balanced as it is with the unions and management asking peers to assess the names presented. Indeed, that scrutiny may be easy for the employer as a repeat participant in the process, handling numerous complaints from dissatisfied employees. But it is unlikely to apply to the claimant for whom the case is presumably the first experience with arbitration and arbitrators. The claimant's representative, if an attorney, will likewise have had limited experience in the selection of arbitrators, and thus may be unfamiliar with the prior users or experience of those arbitrators on the list. That is why the *Protocol* proposed listing the names of recent users of the arbitrators' services, so that both parties would have access to information about the panelists' backgrounds, opinions, and effectiveness in conducting arbitration hearings.

Section B3 of the *Protocol* provides: "We also recommend that prior to selection of an arbitrator each side should be provided with the names, addresses, and phone numbers of representatives of that arbitrator's six most recent cases to aid them in selection."

The parties over a period of time probably could agree on an arbitrator by themselves. But the adversarial nature of the procedure, the desire for an arbitrator who is trained and acceptable to the regulatory agency, and the uncertainty of an award from an unknown and untrained arbitrator have all made parties reluctant to make the attempt. At this early stage it has resulted in greater reliance on appointing agencies like the AAA or J.A.M.S./Endispute than was common in the early stages of union-management arbitration. Due process commitments enhance these organizations' role as neutral facilitator. Even more than in the union-management field, potential users of arbitration services find it useful to entrust the recruitment and development of a roster of arbitrators, stressing neutrality, experience, and demographic needs, to an outside agency. The designating agencies cull out those whose credibility is challengeable or who are engaged in conflicts of interest. They also facilitate and administer the training programs, insulate against the reuser tilt by handling the designation of arbitrators from the panel for the individual cases, list on the panel cards the arbitrators' training in the various statutes and procedures, and protect against an undue financial influence on the arbitrator by negotiating the parties' relative shares of the arbitrator's fee. By fulfilling these functions, the organizations exercise a neutral role welcomed by the adversaries. This also bolsters the neutrality of the arbitrators on their rosters. Designating an arbitrator for a particular case is most sensitive. Claimants are aware of the potential for rigged procedures where the employer alone assembles the panel from which the claimant is permitted to select an arbitrator, or where the employer unilaterally selects the arbitrator. These arrangements are in marked contrast to a plan under which the parties have access to a cadre of arbitrators they have used before or have approved for designation through a neutral agency.

The AAA and the FMCS in the union-management field are credible in assembling panels and providing them to the parties for mutual selection. The system works where an ongoing role of the parties is to monitor a regular body of neutrals, their decisions, and the frequency of their selection. It also works because the parties' networks place the union-management arbitrator in relative parity between the parties as to the likelihood of rehire. Since union and management share the arbitrator's bill as well as future rehire decisions, there is little economic benefit for the arbitrator to tilt to either side for future work. Indeed, the perception of such a tilt might be sufficient to reduce future selection by these parties or those with whom they network about the arbitrator.

There is a different situation in the nonunion employment field. The claimant's representative cannot monitor and investigate as effectively through word of mouth within an organization as do the unions in the union-management field. Efficiency and avoidance of the reuser tilt can best be achieved by the designating agency distributing the cases as broadly as possible. This can be done by authorizing the designating agency or the government agency to appoint the arbitrator or by rotating the work among the panel. Such a procedure would place a premium on periodically reviewing and cleansing the list and placing new names on it. To provide a role for both the employer and the claimant in selection, while endorsing rotation, the designating agency could select from among the full roster panels of three for each case from which each party would strike one, the surviving member serving as the arbitrator.

To accommodate to these problems, the *Protocol* adopted the following Section C3:

> Upon request of the parties the designating agency should utilize a list procedure such as that of the AAA or select a panel composed of an odd number of mediators and arbitrators from its roster or pool. The panel cards for such individuals should be submitted to the parties for their perusal prior to alternate striking of the names on the list, resulting in the designation of the remaining mediator and/or arbitrator.
>
> The selection process could empower the designating agency to appoint a mediator and/or arbitrator if the striking procedure is unacceptable or unsuccessful.

Discovery

Collective-bargaining arbitration procedures have built-in discovery through the parties' negotiated grievance procedure. They also have the expectation—not always realized—that all relevant information will be presented during those steps to facilitate settlement and avoid appeal to arbitration. In theory at least, nothing new should be presented at the arbitration step. Some agreements even prohibit the presentation of tardy evidence, so as to encourage earlier disclosure. Arbitrators on occasion decline to accept evidence that a party had requested but had been refused at the lower steps of the procedure.

A different dynamic occurs in the statutory area. There is no such grievance procedure. There may be no in-house discovery process prior to arbitration. Instead, the standard procedure for eliciting information prior to litigation usually involves the agency's preliminary investigation and the traditional devices of deposition and discovery. Those devices are particularly important in securing information for the claimant that is uniquely and traditionally within the control of the employer. In litigation these procedures are routine, and used extensively—if not excessively. In some employer-promulgated arbitration systems there are restrictions on the number and length of depositions and on the amount of permitted discovery. One of the crucial benefits of due process is to eliminate arbitrary caps on discovery and depositions to assure that there is reasonable access to both as essential tools to assure expeditious arbitration hearings and hearing preparation. Discovery is an important vehicle to help level the arbitration playing field by assuring the claimant access to information that otherwise would be solely within the employer's domain. On the other hand, there is need to protect against abusive use of both devices because of cost and time. Accordingly, the designated arbitrator should be the one to determine whether either process is being abused, and should be able to rule on the admissibility of the evidence collected. The pertinent provision of the *Protocol* on access to such information, Section B3, provides as follows: "Adequate but limited pre-trial discovery is to be encouraged and employees should have access to all information reasonably relevant to mediation and/or arbitration of their claims. The employee's representative should also have reasonable pre-hearing and hearing access to all such information and documentation.

"Necessary pre-hearing depositions consistent with the expedited nature of arbitration should be available."

Compensation

By its very origins, employer-promulgated arbitration of statutory issues pits the individual claimant against the enterprise. Those employers who unilaterally established unfair arbitration systems did so because they had the deep-pocket resources to fund such a procedure—and were alert to the fact that their challenging employees did not. That disparity led to the abuses of power and the more recent movement to instill due process in such procedures. Essential to that due process is assuring adequate compensation for those implementing the system without permitting the funder to control the outcome. Compensation affects due process in two areas: compensation for the claimant's representative and compensation for the neutral.

Compensation for Claimant's Representative

Our judicial system anticipates that claimants and defendants will either represent themselves or will secure representation, usually by attorneys, and that the financial arrangements for representation are matters of the parties' concern. In many cases counsel will be provided by the court when parties lack the financial resources. Reimbursement for representational expenses may be sought as part of any financial compensation awarded at the outcome of such proceedings. In collective-bargaining arbitration, the funding arrangements are different: the employee is represented by the union, or its lawyer designee, paid for out of union dues. In claims before government agencies, representation is usually provided by the agency staff itself, making claims of discrimination under Title VII, for example, free of cost to the claimants. In some cases claimants seek their own attorneys to process the claims and proceed in court with such representation. It is not uncommon for the plaintiff's bar to work on a contingency arrangement, requiring some initial payment as a retainer but deferring the bulk of the fee until conclusion of the case. At that point the representative benefits only if there is money provided in a favorable award. The traditional employer-promulgated arbitration system anticipates that claimants will either proceed pro se or fund representation on their own. As noted earlier, in a few systems, such as that in place at Brown & Root, the employer makes provision for subsidy of attorney fees for the claimant. Such outlay does provide representation to make the procedure more balanced and fair. It also encourages use of the system in lieu of more costly court proceedings and reduces the likelihood of later challenge on procedural grounds.

Since the right to counsel and representation is such a vital element of our due process tradition, any private arbitration of statutory rights should provide the right to representation. That is particularly important when one is processing claims for low-wage-earners who would otherwise have little resources for attorney fees and whose claims might be too small to attract interest of contingency fee attorneys. It is in the self-interest of employers providing such systems to provide financial assistance in this area, both to assure the efficient operation of the systems they create and to demonstrate to their other employees that the systems anticipate fair proceedings with adequate due process protection. The MCAD procedures, in addition to providing staff, provide representation to pro se claimants under employer-promulgated systems. The Commission may also recruit outside counsel for an individual or encourage other organizations (such as women's groups, civil rights organizations, or unions) to serve as counsel. Some outside funding might also be available for such legal assistance.

The *Protocol* encourages employer subsidy to claimants for representation in Section B2. "The amount and method of payment for representation should be determined between the claimant and the representative. We recommend, however, a number of existing systems which provide employer reimbursement of at least a portion of the employee's attorney fees, especially for lower paid employees. The arbitrator should have the authority to provide for fee reimbursement, in whole or in part, as part of the remedy in accordance with applicable law or in the interests of justice."

Compensation of the Arbitrator

Compensation for the arbitrator in the union-management field is based on the two parties equally sharing the arbitrator's fees and expenses, unless some other arrangement is negotiated between them.[4] Equal sharing is the best deterrent, if there is one, against the arbitrator favoring the client most likely to provide future work.

But equal sharing in the employment law field imposes an unfair burden on the claimant, particularly for low-income employees. Shielding the arbitrator from knowing the source of compensation may be the most promising method of payment to protect against bias in favor of future reemployment. The agency can then negotiate as close to equal sharing as possible, but at least the arbitrator can function with the fiction that the parties have shared in the cost.

Due process also requires that new neutrals be protected from the pressures inherent in seeking to establish themselves as professionally acceptable in this new field. In the union-management field it is assumed that the union and management representatives have their respective networks for information to help them in the selection of arbitrators for future work. Additionally, the practice of equally sharing arbitrator's fees provides monitoring and control to weed out those who place self-interest, or indeed greed, above their obligations as neutral decision makers. The weeding-out process has concentrated the work among a core group of arbitrators in collective bargaining disputes, those trusted as fair by the disputing parties. In the statutory field at this stage, there is no comparable parity in selection. Multiple attorneys or representatives will be handling individual claims and individual selections of arbitrators. Arbitrators eager to achieve career standing, or even merely more work, might be likely to tilt in favor of the deep-pocket reuser. More work is likely to come from the employer than from any single employee, even if the parties equally shared the arbitrator's fee. To minimize any proclivity to issue awards based on the prospect of future rehires, the *Protocol* in Section C6 proposed as a safeguard that the designating agency pay the arbitrator without the arbitrator knowing whether the source of the funding was solely the employer or both parties under some shared arrangement with contributions from the employee and perhaps even the statutory agency: "Impartiality is best assured by the parties sharing the fees of the mediator and arbitrator. In cases where the economic condition of a party does not permit equal sharing, the parties should make mutually acceptable arrangements to achieve that goal if at all possible. In the absence of such agreement, the arbitrator should determine allocation of fees. The designating agency by negotiating the parties' share of costs and collecting such fees, might be able to reduce the bias potential of disparate contributions by forwarding payment to the mediator and/or arbitrator without disclosing the parties' share therein."

Arbitrator's Hearing Authority

The area in which there is clearest transfer from the union-management arena to employment arbitration is in the scope of the arbitrator's authority to conduct the hearing. Indeed, in the nonunion sector adoption of the authority traditionally ascribed to a union-management arbitrator is even more crucial, given the disparity of power between the parties, the absence of any grievance procedure for discovery, and the arbitrator's greater authority over the award and remedy. Arbitrators in the statutory area have the heavier burden of functioning as the substitute for the government agencies in assuring due process during the course of the hearing and providing a forum comparable to that of the agencies and the courts in terms of protecting statutory rights. The broad scope of that authority is synthesized in Section C5 of the *Protocol*: "The arbitrator should be bound by applicable agreements, statutes, regulations and rules of procedure of the designating agency, including the authority to determine the time and place of the hearing, permit reasonable discovery, issue subpoenas, decide arbitrability issues, preserve order, and privacy in the hearings, rule on evidentiary matters, determine the close of the hearing and procedures for post hearing submissions and issue an award resolving the submitted dispute."

Scope of Review

The concept of arbitration as an effective substitute for statutory agencies and the courts assumes that the agencies and the courts, as the present determiners of statutory conformity, give full faith and credit to the results of the arbitrator's determinations. In light of *Gilmer*, the federal courts seem quite willing to refrain from any critical review of the due process or the statutory fealty of an arbitrator's award. One would hope that the courts would undertake greater scrutiny of employment arbitration decisions to assure that arbitration systems do provide due process protections, that there is adequate consideration of the statutes and regulations to support the view that arbitration is indeed merely a substitution of forum, and to give society some measure of faith in the judiciary as the ultimate safeguard of basic statutory rights.

Certainly the administrative and statutory agencies must be cautious in ceding full authority to the arbitrator for fear that the decision may not only be at partial variance with the law, but worse, may be so contrary to the law as to violate the *Spielberg-Olin* standard of deferral relied upon by the NLRB. The adoption of similar standards by the MCAD for review of cases submitted to arbitration under its aegis holds out the promise that the Commission will consider intervention and rejection of arbitration awards deemed repugnant to the statutes it enforces. The provisions of the *Protocol* on this issue read as follows: "The arbitrator should be empowered to award whatever relief would be available in court under the law. The arbitrator should issue an opinion and award setting forth a summary of the issues, including the type(s) of dispute(s), the damages and/or other relief requested and awarded, a statement of any other issues resolved and a statement regarding the disposition of any statutory claim(s)."

Summary

Formulation of due process standards is not done lightly or quickly. It has taken our legal institutions since the Magna Carta to develop the standards of due process and legal fairness to which we believe all citizens should be entitled. The deprivation of those standards in certain management-promulgated systems raises the question of what due process protections are missing or should be provided to employees bound by such systems. Participants in the union-management field have developed, over the last century, what might be viewed as an efficient arrangement acceptable to both parties, the NLRB, and the courts. The *Protocol* sought to chronicle those concepts in the hope that they provide an acceptable model to assure that due process is provided in ADR systems.

Although the emphasis of the procedures might appear to be on arbitration rather than on mediation, it must be remembered that the most effective mediation usually occurs against the backdrop of imminent arbitration. In that sense, the *Protocol* strengthens mediation as an essential element in reaching resolution of these disputes. The basic elements set forth in this chapter constitute the first step in trying to bring fairness and equity to workplace disputes that have not always been governed by these principles.

Chapter Seven

Alternative Dispute Resolution in Government Agencies

Until the major organizations affecting the workplace accept common or congruent policies, a voluntary system of dispute resolution cannot operate effectively and fairly in the area of employment law and regulations. First, state and federal administrative agencies need to specify orders and regulations to implement employment statutes and develop standards for adjudicating individual cases. Businesses and other organizations providing employment need to accept the system, as do labor unions, civil rights and women's groups, and other organizations that influence and represent the views of workers on voluntary dispute resolution. And the courts, which determine whether voluntary dispute resolution programs provide due process in the circumstances and whether awards are in conformance with law, need to share in the general agreement. Each of these areas poses significant issues and problems.

This chapter initially discusses the issues and attitudes in government administrative agencies that have limited their resort to ADR processes and negotiated rulemaking. It then turns to the beginnings of ADR in state[1] and federal agencies treating employment law. Chapter Eight will take up the Massachusetts Commission Against Discrimination as a case study in the adoption of mediation and arbitration to resolve cases under statute.

The Administrative Dispute Resolution Act,[2] enacted in 1990, authorized and encouraged federal agencies to use ADR to resolve disputes. The statute by its terms sunset and lapsed on October 1, 1995. A successor statute, without the limitations of a sunset provision, was signed into law on October 19, 1996.[3]

In Section 2 of the 1990 Act, Congress made a series of findings that explain and support the resort to other means to adjudicate disputes than resort to administrative tribunals and the courts. These findings are so fundamental to the present volume that it is worth quoting them at length:

1. Administrative procedures, as embodied in chapter 5 of title 5, United States Code . . . [are] intended to offer a prompt, expert, and inexpensive means of resolving disputes as an alternative to litigation in the Federal courts;

2. Administrative proceedings have become increasingly formal, costly, and lengthy resulting in unnecessary expenditures of time and in a decreased likelihood of achieving consensual resolution of disputes;

3. Alternative means of dispute resolution have been used in the private sector for many years and, in appropriate circumstances, have yielded decisions that are faster, less expensive, and less contentious;

4. Such alternative means can lead to more creative, efficient, and sensible outcomes;

5. Such alternative means may be used advantageously in a wide variety of administrative programs;

6. Explicit authorization of the use of well-tested dispute resolution techniques will eliminate ambiguity of agency authority under existing law;

7. Federal agencies may not only receive the benefit of techniques that were developed in the private sector, but may also take the lead in the further development and refinement of such techniques; and

8. The availability of a wide range of dispute resolution procedures, and an increased understanding of the most effective use of such procedures, will enhance the operation of the Government and better serve the public.

ADR is defined to include the following methods of dispute resolution:[4] settlement negotiations, conciliation, facilitation, mediation, fact-finding, minitrials, and arbitration, or any combination of these processes. This broad view of ADR, which includes arbitration, is at variance with the usage of the FMCS, which states "the terms mediation and Alternative Dispute Resolution (ADR) have become nearly synonymous."[5]

This chapter is divided into six sections. The first discusses the constitutionality of private arbitration in adjudication under regulations. The next four cover agency procedures as an impediment, types of cases precluded from arbitration, standards for arbitration awards, and bureaucratic restraints. The last traces current ADR efforts that have begun to appear in state and federal agencies.

Constitutionality of Private Arbitration

The 1990 statute explicitly authorized binding arbitration[6] but provided, in a one-sided manner, that the administrative agency could terminate the proceedings or vacate the award on thirty days notice before the award became final. This reservation clearly served as a disincentive to the development of arbitration.

The Administrative Conference of the United States (ACUS) reported that this provision (Section 580-c) was included "to accommodate Department of Justice concern over the constitutionality of binding an agency through a decision made by someone who is not an 'officer of the United States.'" The ACUS stated it did not and does not share the 1989 concern of the Department of Justice.[7] In February 1995, the ABA recommended by resolution that this thirty-day agency escape clause provision be eliminated from the statute.

The concerns over the constitutionality of voluntary agreements to arbitrate on the part of the government were raised by then-Assistant Attorney General William Barr, who testified before congressional committees in 1989 that the Appointments Clause[8] of the Constitution would prohibit the government from entering into binding arbitration. The Appointments Clause sets forth the exclusive mechanisms by which an officer of the United States may be appointed. If an arbitrator were to be deemed an officer of the United States, then the appointment could only be made as prescribed by the Appointments Clause.

In 1995, the Department of Justice stated that the views expressed by William Barr in 1989 had been superseded by its memorandum of September 7, 1995, which held that "there are no constitutional impediments preventing federal agencies from voluntarily engaging in the use of binding arbitration."[9] This memorandum held that arbitrators are "manifest private actors who are, at most, independent contractors to rather than employees of, the federal government. . . . Because arbitrators are not officers, the Appointments Clause does not place any requirements or restrictions on the manner in which they are chosen."

The constitutionality cloud over government participation in arbitration has been lifted. On February 7, 1996, President Clinton issued Executive Order 12988, Civil Justice Reform, encouraging resort to ADR explicitly including "private arbitration and other forms of private dispute resolution" in appropriate cases.[10] Further, as noted earlier, the Administrative Dispute Resolution Act of 1996 eliminated the agency thirty-day escape clause provision.

Legislated Agency Procedures as an Impediment to ADR

Over the past sixty years, largely relying on its constitutional authority to regulate interstate commerce, Congress has enacted almost two hundred statutes vastly expanding the federal regulation of the workplace. This expansion was concentrated in three periods: 1931–1940 (illustrated by the Fair Labor Standards Act and the National Labor Relations Act), 1963–1974 (including Title VII of the Civil Rights Act, OSHA, and the Employee Retirement Income Security Act), and 1986–1993 (including the Americans with Disabilities Act, the Employee Polygraph Protection Act, and the Family and Medical Leave Act).[11] This complex regulatory framework for the American workplace, legislated in administrations of both Republicans and Democrats, has been a shifting complex that changes from time to time as a result of congressional measures, agency orders and rules, review commission actions, and judicial interpretations. Employers also face a combination of federal and state laws that may involve federal dominance or preemption, dual control with varying degrees of authority, or a defined federal-state partnership.

In the process of expansion of statutory regulation over the years, Congress generally designed a distinctive process of adjudication within each statute. The processes of inspection, complaint, decision making, and review and appeal, and the rights to jury trial and even access or resort to the courts, are not uniform among employment statutes administered by the Labor Department or the EEOC.

There is no common procedure within these agencies of the subordinate offices charged with the administration of separate statutes. Moreover, after years of discussion, there is not even a common database within the Department of Labor or the EEOC to identify and track different types of cases involving the same employer. The simple fact is that the statutory evolution of workplace regulation, with distinctive administrative processes specified in each law, has hampered an overall simplification or standardization of dispute resolution.

This diversity complicates the design of any ADR system that might be used in place of the specified statutory procedures, including resort to the courts. It may well be said that the complex statutory differences enhance the role and power of each bureaucratic niche, insulating many of them even from top agency policymakers.

A few illustrations are in order. Under the Fair Labor Standards Act and the Employee Polygraph Protection Act, either individuals or the Department of Labor may file cases in the federal courts seeking review of adjudication of the statute or regulations or redress for violations. Under OSHA, on the other hand, only the agency may seek compliance through the courts after it files a complaint against an employer. OSHA complaints, unlike Wage and Hour cases, may be reviewed by a commission that is independent of the Secretary of Labor.

Statutes differ in their applicability to smaller enterprises, varyingly defined. As illustrations, OSHA provides in its injury and illness log for an exemption of ten or less employees; the Worker Adjustment and Retraining Notification Act (WARN) specifies workplaces of a hundred or more; the Americans with Disabilities Act does not apply to employers with fewer than fifteen employees; the Age Discrimination in Employment Act has twenty as the minimum number of employees for coverage; and the Fair Labor Standards Act provides various dollar-volume-of-business exemptions. Moreover, the Small Business Regulatory Enforcement Fairness Act of 1996[12] has complicated the tasks of applying employment law standards to "small business" without any size or dollar-volume definitions of what constitutes small business.

This Act finds that government agencies have too often placed greater "regulatory burdens on small entities than necessitated by statute." The Act creates a structure of Regional Small Business Regulatory Fairness Boards and a national ombudsman in the Small Business Administration to receive reports of "excessive enforcement actions of agencies against small business." It provides for the submission of proposed agency rules and regulations affecting small business to each house of the Congress and to the comptroller, and it provides for specialized judicial proceedings. The impact of these declarations and procedures on the regulatory and adjudication processes of agencies at this stage is uncertain and highly complex.

Some statutory procedures involve relatively small potential damages for violations, as typically in the case of the Family and Medical Leave Act, while others, as in the pension issues of the Employee Retirement Income Security Act, generally involve more substantial sums. Some statutes provide for jury trials, others do not; some include punitive damages while others do not. Some statutes provide for review in either state or federal courts, while others are confined to the federal courts. There are various provisions regarding attorneys' fees.[13]

There should be no necessary inference that these statutory differences are necessarily unwarranted or ill suited to the problems the particular pieces of legislation sought to address and remedy. Rather, the complex legislated structures are very different and not automatically or uniformly well suited to ADR methods, and particularly to arbitration. The separate question arises, apart from the introduction of ADR methods, whether legislated provision should be developed for a greater standardization and coordination of these diverse procedures treating American employees, workers, labor organizations, and workplaces. Common procedures within the Labor Department or the EEOC are conceivable; a tripartite review body could be helpful in shaping practical regulation; the court review could be concentrated in a specialized circuit court; or—for a more fundamental change—a European-type labor court could be established. The issues in such changes need to be addressed, but these questions are beyond the scope of this volume.

The issues that are of central concern here are rather which statutory programs, particularly at the outset, can be most appropriately selected for experimentation with ADR, including mediation and arbitration? At what stage in the prescribed process of a case—initial complaint, investigation, probable cause, hearing, settlement discussion, decision to take the case to court, and so on— is a qualified neutral to be introduced (by voluntary agreement of the agency and the parties) to resolve the differences by mediation or arbitration? And what types of cases should be excluded, and at what points in the process, from access to ADR methods?

Cases Unsuitable for Arbitration

If ADR methods, including arbitration, are to grow as applied to employment law, the administrative agencies at the department level will require broad discretion in specifying types of cases to be reserved for the traditional methods of agency adjudication followed by resort to the courts. It is no serious restriction on the development of ADR methods to recognize that, particularly at the outset, not every case or issue is suitable for voluntary mediation and arbitration. These reservations will probably be based on the following factors:

1. Some cases or issues represent critical or central questions in the development of statutory interpretation and policy. The conventional statutory process is more likely to be appropriate for setting such precedents.

2. Some cases may have significant impact on persons or organizations that are not parties to the immediate dispute, so that a conventional proceeding or enlarged arbitration may be more appropriate for the issues and precedents involved than two-party arbitration.

3. Some cases may involve an ongoing congressional concern with an issue so that the agency may need a continuing involvement in a question.

4. Some cases may potentially involve a criminal violation of law and be inappropriate for private arbitration.

5. Finally, as a matter of policy, the agency should refuse to recognize a commitment to arbitration as a condition of employment, or otherwise imposed prior to a specific dispute.[14]

But these and other restraints on the application of ADR methods, including arbitration, still provide a wide range of cases for the experimentation and development of private mediation and arbitration of employment law disputes.

Standards for Arbitration Awards

Just as there have developed a few restraints, widely recognized, on the arbitrator and arbitration award in the practice of labor-management arbitration under collective bargaining agreements, so would it be expected that comparable restraints apply to private mediation and arbitration of employment law adjudication. The system would probably provide that administrative agencies or courts would vacate awards only under conditions like these:

1. The award was procured by fraud, duress, or dishonesty.

2. The award was tainted by the prejudicial misconduct of the arbitrator or a party, or by an undisclosed conflict of interest.

3. The award exceeded the authority of the arbitrator.

4. The award was otherwise contrary to law.

Restraints from the Agency Bureaucracy

The process of changing the long-time procedures of well-established government agencies and their staffs has always been slow and difficult. The application of ADR to the adjudication of employment law disputes is certain to be no different.

As noted earlier, the Labor Department began to experiment with negotiated rulemaking in 1975. Various statutes, executive orders, and secretaries have endorsed the approach, but in the past twenty years, the Department has used this method for no more than four or five of its hundreds of orders and regulations. With the assistance of the FMCS and the ACUS, the Department also developed a highly successful pilot test program of mediation in the adjudication of cases awaiting litigation in the Philadelphia Region in 1992. The experience was carefully evaluated, noting the savings in time and costs. Labor Department participants independently concluded that the settlements were at least comparable to the likely outcome of litigation. But there was no follow-up of this evaluated success.

It is essential to understand what lies behind such inertia and resistance to new methods. This subtheme might be entitled the restraints on innovation in government agencies—or one might refer to the well-known judgment of Niccolò Machiavelli in *The Prince*: "There is nothing more difficult to handle, more doubtful of success, and more dangerous to carry through than initiating changes in a state's constitution."

In the Labor Department, agencies such as Wage and Hour and OSHA are charged with developing regulations, inspections, and findings of apparent violations of statutes and regulations. These cases are turned over to the solicitor's office, in field offices or later nationally, and divided along the lines of the operating agencies for disposition, settlement, or litigation. These roles are relatively segmented. The senior personnel of the legal staff are long-term civil servants, dedicated to their assignments. They have little direct experience with the workplace or with worker-management or labor-management relations or with mediation or arbitration.

They believe that employment laws and their regulations are designed to assure workers of the prescribed standards, that the government has the duty to enforce these standards in all cases, and that the employees affected by violations should not be required to contribute financially to any enforcement. They claim that outside arbitrators and mediators cannot know the statutes and regulations as well as the department's legal staff, and these outsiders are suspect. The existing procedures have been the established order for many years; they have served well and they should remain unchanged. In this view, the current approach includes nothing that is broken and needs to be fixed.

The legal staff does not understand why parties should choose to enter into arbitration: Most of them feel that such arbitration may suggest to the employer that the Department is not that interested in litigating the case. To the employee it may appear the person is giving up the free resources of the government and would be required to pay the costs to achieve the same goal. The employer might also be concerned that the Department might seek to overturn the arbitrator's decision.

The legal bureaucracy has been unable to resolve the dilemma posed by the operating agencies, which are deeply concerned that caseloads are increasing at the same time that budgets and staffing are declining and are projected to continue to decline. The resort to ADR methods does not appear to many in the present legal staff to be a legitimate response.[15]

It is abundantly clear that any widespread resort to ADR methods, including mediation and arbitration, will require extensive retraining of personnel—currently experienced only in litigation—in the methods and procedures of ADR. An active leadership focus on these methods and on staff training is indispensable in agencies preoccupied with conventional methods in a time of sharply declining funding and staff resources.

A cost analysis was conducted by a separate unit in the Labor Department for three proposed pilot arbitration programs, announced for comment on February 12, 1997, that applied the same methodology that had been used in the cost-benefit review of the Philadelphia region ADR Pilot Project.[16] The voluntary private arbitration pilot proposal, it was estimated, would result in over a 40 percent cost savings per case and a reduction in adjudication time of 50 percent. The availability of such potential results warrants experimentation with mediation and arbitration on a selected basis.

Beginnings of ADR in State and Federal Agencies

Workers' Compensation Arbitration

Since 1991, starting with Massachusetts, a number of states have authorized unions and employers (parties to collective bargaining agreements) to bargain over specific features of workers' compensation, including a panel of doctors to treat injured workers, the doctors to conduct medical-legal evaluations, the vocational rehabilitation counselors to advise injured workers and alternative methods of dispute resolution. In these respects the parties are allowed partially to opt out of state-run workers' compensation plans and create a private adjudicatory procedure. As of 1997, nine states had enacted such legislation.[17] The standards of benefits prescribed in the state workers' compensation plans continue to apply to these carved-out provisions.

The privatization of the selection of a panel of doctors and the dispute resolution process through jointly selected arbitrators was initiated in the construction industry, which typically has had very high workers' compensation costs. The first parties to adopt these features were Bechtel Construction Company and the Pioneer Valley Building and Construction Trades Council on a western Massachusetts project. These construction agreements typically specify added measures the parties undertake to reduce accidents and enhance health care and safety.

The workers' compensation section of an agreement provides as follows:

All employees working under this Agreement shall be covered as required by the Massachusetts Workers' Compensation Act (hereinafter "the Act"). However, recognizing the need to reduce the number and severity of accidents and to provide an efficient and effective method for dealing with disputes resulting from compensable personal injuries and occupational diseases, the parties agree to utilize the provisions of Chapter 152 of the General Laws of the Commonwealth to establish a system of dispute prevention and resolution as a substitute for the conciliation, conference, hearing and review processes of the Division of Industrial Accidents. In addition, as more fully described below, the parties will endeavor to broaden and improve this process to include better access to and delivery of medical care for employees affected by occupational injury or disease and to review the appropriate level of benefits and benefit conditions as permitted. All parties including contractors, unions and employees recognize the value of an efficient, timely workers' compensation system. They agree that abuses of the system will not be tolerated, and will cooperate in any investigation of a claim or abuse.[18]

The testimony of parties under such agreements is that health and safety performance has been improved, costs have been reduced, and workers have had quick and high-quality access to medical care. The State of California reported that in 1995 6.9 million person hours of construction labor and $157.6 million in wages were covered by carved-out workers' compensation programs. The incurred losses appear to be less than expected and the ADR provisions are working well, but there was some concern over the lists of medical providers.[19]

These new developments need to be studied and appraised when sufficient experience has been accumulated. But it should not be unexpected that all parties to a collective bargaining agreement may benefit when they work together to enhance health and safety on the job, to provide prompt and high-quality care, and to reduce the time and extent of disputes over workers' compensation.

Labor Department Agencies

Following the release of the Report and Recommendations of the Commission on the Future of Worker-Management Relations in January 1995, the Labor Department established a task force comprising representatives of the principal operating agencies, the policy analysis unit, and the solicitor's office to explore the potentials of mediation and arbitration in the resolution of disputes over employment statutes it administers. The greatest interest and potential appeared to be in the Employment Standards Administration and in OSHA. The Mine Safety and Health Administration was in the process of working out its own program, called Alternative Case Resolution Initiatives.[20]

The objective of the task force was to select a limited number of pilot programs into which voluntary mediation and arbitration could be introduced so that the experience could be carefully evaluated, and if appropriate, extended in time to other programs. In February 1997, the Department proposed for comment an expanded use of voluntary mediation or arbitration in a pilot test of six categories of cases.[21] In general, these categories included whistleblower cases under various statutes, certain cases arising under the Family and Medical Leave Act and the Fair Labor Standards Act, and other specified issues. The Department also used this notice in the *Federal Register* to experiment with the electronic filing of comments on proposed regulations.

EEOC

The development of ADR procedures in the EEOC since 1992, primarily involving mediation, is briefly described in Chapter Three. In 1996, the EEOC entered into an agreement with the

FMCS for reimbursement from its budget to implement external mediation and to train EEOC staff in selected district offices.

In early 1997, Chairman Casellas stated he is "committed" to getting ADR "as fully implemented as EEOC can."ADR is not a "panacea" to eliminate the large EEOC backlog but "it can help." Casellas said he is "frustrated by some resistance, although not widespread or prevalent," among EEOC staff and commissioners. "There remains this culture of litigation [that believes] the only way to be effective is to litigate."[22] These attitudes of agency lawyers correspond to the resistance reported earlier in the Labor Department. Casellas stated that while some cases may require litigation, there are hundreds and hundreds of cases that could benefit from ADR and for which its use would in no way be antithetical to the enforcement of civil rights laws.

Federal Labor Relations Authority

The core mission of this agency is to resolve cases and help parties provide interest-based conflict resolution services in pending unfair labor practice, representation, negotiability, and impasse bargaining disputes involving federal employees. In early 1996, the agency announced a new ADR program dedicated "to reducing the costs of conflict in the federal workplace by improving labor-management relationships and encouraging alternative methods of resolving conflict."[23]

Federal Mediation and Conciliation Service

The FMCS dates its involvement in ADR to the early 1970s, when it mediated a land dispute between the Navajo and Hopi Indian tribes. It facilitated negotiated rulemaking in the 1980s in the Federal Aviation Administration. The Administrative Dispute Resolution Act of 1990 authorized FMCS to make its services available to federal, state, and local governmental bodies and agencies.

The agency reported in the fall 1996 that since fiscal year 1990 it had "entered into more than 300 interagency agreements to provide ADR services to federal and state agencies." The role of the FMCS in the 1992 experiment in the Philadelphia Region of the Labor Department and the 1996 agreement with the EEOC have been noted earlier.

The FMCS seeks to promote ADR (identified with mediation) by designing systems of dispute resolution for government agencies, by education and training of agencies' staff, by facilitating negotiated rulemaking, and by evaluation of ADR programs in agencies. In each of its districts, one field mediator has been designated to coordinate ADR activity; it maintains a national office of ADR Services.[24] These services have expanded as the traditional labor-management dispute workload of the agency has declined.

While stand-alone mediation, assistance in negotiated rule-making, and staff training make a contribution to federal and state agencies in the development of alternatives to litigation, arbitration by outside neutrals and related mediation is the indispensable element to ADR in employment law disputes. Moreover, given the diversity and complexities of statutes and regulations, neutrals need a significant degree of specialized training and experience to be effective in employment law disputes. A general purpose mediator or arbitrator has limitations. Yet the FMCS has a useful contribution to make in the development of ADR, particularly in the training of staffs of agencies experienced in litigation to appreciate the potential of alternative methods of dispute resolution.

Summary

Widespread dissatisfaction has developed in the public sector as well as in private workplaces over the costs and delays involved in the processes of adjudication of employment law disputes by administrative agencies and the courts. There is likewise widespread experimentation with ADR methods, principally voluntary mediation and arbitration. Among the impediments to change in the directions of ADR and arbitration are the complex procedures of each of several hundred statutes that provide specialized adjudication, only some of which are readily or uniformly adapted to ADR, and the inertia and restraints of the legal bureaucracy in the agencies.

Despite these obstacles, a number of fruitful experimental programs are under way in the EEOC, the Department of Labor, and other federal agencies, on occasion with the assistance of the FMCS. Programs are also under way in the Massachusetts Commission Against Discrimination (described in Chapter Eight) and in some states in dispute resolution of workers' compensation benefits under collective bargaining agreements. All these experiments will in due course require careful evaluation and reports.

These growth buds within administrative agencies, along with employer-sponsored programs and the amended rules and training activities of appointing agencies such as the AAA, represent the beginnings of areas of ADR in employment law that need to be encouraged and perfected. They will never displace all conventional employment law adjudication, but they should make it easier for administrative agencies to concentrate on their more significant cases and policy issues.

Chapter Eight

A Case Study in System Design

The Massachusetts Commission
Against Discrimination

The development of mediation and arbitration systems can help reduce the costs and delay of traditional litigation. These advantages are particularly notable in discrimination cases, but meeting the procedural and substantive standards prescribed by legislation presents both a challenge and opportunity for ADR. Federal and state agencies responsible for enforcing civil rights legislation often resist such changes as threats to their mission. The EEOC leadership takes the position that the agency needs to handle cases where a "pattern or practice of discrimination" exists since it alone has the experience and authority to root out embedded discrimination beyond the concerns of an individual employee.

The constituencies who fought for civil rights legislation for thirty years are not about to surrender their gains to procedures appearing to dilute the enforcement power of the agencies. Indeed they fought for legislation and the right to trial by jury precisely to avoid the prejudice of individual judges, making resort to arbitration a throwback to imposed decisions without community evaluation and control. Some groups may view any change in the procedure for resolving discrimination claims as an encroachment on their access to juries and the potential for lucrative judgments in the courts. The overwhelming evidence in the past few years, however, is that agency caseloads are increasing while their budgets remain relatively stagnant or shrink. The painful reality is that many of these cases are not being resolved, that the growing backlog means years of uncertainty and, at best, delayed justice. Large jury verdicts are few and far between—and usually apply to claims of executives and high-paid employees. These judgments benefit the average employee by serving as well-publicized deterrents and offering some hope of changing unacceptable discriminatory behavior, but they do not reflect the experience of the bulk of plaintiffs in discrimination cases.

The evidence suggests that mediation and arbitration for routine cases may well create an appreciation of the processes and open the door to increased attention by agencies to claimant representatives in nonroutine cases. The National Employment Lawyers Association and the ACLU, as signatories to the *Protocol*, are also concerned with assuring claimants due process. Some managements suspect the *Protocol* procedures as intruding on their unilateral authority to create arbitration procedures under the *Gilmer* decision. But management representatives in the *Protocol* process also expressed their commitment to assure that such procedures are fair and consistent with due process requirements. The endorsement of *Protocol* standards by the J.A.M.S./Endispute and the AAA has isolated employers who do not want to assure fairness while encouraging employers to follow standards of fairness that now have broad support in the employment community.

This chapter discusses the general approach to developing an agency arbitration procedure. It then devotes the rest of its space to discussion of the experience with one program in Massachusetts.

Background and Early Experiments

Those who are committed to the development of structures with due process protections are now more easily able to demonstrate the value of such systems to their skeptical constituencies. There appear to be two main avenues for expanding the use of these due process standards. One is through employer adoption of the standards in their internal machinery or through reliance on designating agencies such as the AAA that have built the *Protocol* into their rules. That approach would appear to have the most promising prospects for rapid and widespread implementation of *Protocol* standards.

The second means of encouraging adoption of the standards is through encouraging the traditional enforcement agencies to offer voluntary mediation and arbitration under these due process standards as an alternative to their lengthy, costly, and public procedures for statutory enforcement. Agency adoption of such privatized alternatives can be accomplished in several ways.

One approach is to marshal all the potential users into developing a structure that is then presented to the agency for its adoption. Such an approach was undertaken in New York State, where the legislature, at the behest of the New York State Bar Association and other groups, passed a law calling for arbitration to reduce the backlog of discrimination cases pending before the Human Rights Commission.[1] With the support of the plaintiff and management bar and the AAA, a structure was developed, and a panel of twenty arbitrators recruited and trained. Then the legislatively created procedure was, in effect, imposed upon the agency for administration. The plan called for arbitration being suggested to the parties in a mailing sent after the probable cause finding. It called for both parties sharing the full cost of the arbitrator, plus the AAA fee, but gave the agency no right of review of the arbitrator's decision.[2] Whether the project was resented by the agency personnel who felt it to be a criticism of their good faith efforts to enforce the statutes with restricted resources, or whether it failed because of its own structured shortcomings, the result has been only two agency cases being arbitrated.

Profiting from that example, a more promising alternative would be to encourage the involvement of the enforcement agency as well as the user groups in the initial development of the plan. This would enable the agency to determine whether such a system meets its needs and goals. With early agency interest and input, it becomes feasible to fashion a structure that has agency support and encouragement and that facilitates the implementation of agency goals.

Establishing the Massachusetts Model

This latter approach was followed to establish the system now operating at the Massachusetts Commission Against Discrimination (MCAD). A chronological recitation may provide some guidance to others interested in establishing similar systems in other jurisdictions.

The initial contact with MCAD resulted from a suggestion to Arnold M. Zack by an EEOC Commissioner that the state agencies, rather than the EEOC itself, would be a better locus for developing an arbitration model. Since Zack comes from Boston, the Commissioner suggested that he approach the then-Chairman of the MCAD, Michael Duffy, to discuss the proposal. Zack met with Duffy on November 20, 1995, providing a copy of the *Protocol*. On November 24, 1995, he wrote Duffy listing the following advantages of arbitration:

1. *Reducing the time taken to closure with a final and binding resolution through arbitration at a date certain.* This would be an expeditious substitute for the long delays, multiple appeals, and the uncertain finality of litigation, and with prospects of rapid resolution, would introduce reinstatement at work as a viable remedy.

2. *Reducing the cost of closure by focusing on a single adversarial proceeding.* This would allow all parties to avoid the financial burden of extensive legal pretrial procedures and extended posttrial appeals.

3. *Saving the Commission money by shifting the cost of enforcement to employers accused of statutory violation in lieu of using Commission funds.* Arbitrators would be authorized to award legal fees as part of their decisions.

4. *Enhancing the Commission's public image.* This would be accomplished by reducing case backlog, expediting case handling, using trained experienced neutrals with public support and taxpayer saving, and avoiding the cost of pursuing cases to full Commission hearing and to the courts.

5. *Enhancing the parties' sense of participation in the process.* They would gain this through joint selection of neutrals of their own choice.

6. *Providing a choice of trained decision makers in lieu of hearings before the commissioners or randomly assigned judges.* Training would be administered by a neutral designating agency and provided by experts in the various discrimination statutes, in remedies and in the procedures of arbitration. Arbitrators would have the same remedy powers as the courts, including the right to assess punitive damages and legal fees. The agency would retain the right to review such decisions to assure against their being repugnant to the statute or palpably wrong, and to reject those awards it finds violated that standard.

7. *Enhancing the role of conciliation and mediation.* The preferred mediatory function would be far more effective when offered against the backdrop of a pending fixed arbitration date and the risk of a final and binding award. Mediation would be provided by neutrals trained in the statutes and the process of mediation.

8. *Encouraging the development of a more persuasive body of case law written by arbitrators and providing the parties with useful guidance for future conduct.* The industrial jurisprudence of collective-bargaining arbitration might be emulated by a similar law of the shop governing workplace statutory conduct. This might have greater reach and impact among employers and potential claimants than more formal Commission or judicial decisions. The parties' desire for privacy could be assured by providing a redacted version of the arbitrator's opinion and award.

The letter to Duffy also set forth recommendations for the features to include in the proposed new structure:

- The employee's right to a representative of the employee's own selection, attorney, civil rights expert, trade union representative. Hopefully the employer would make some contribution to the cost of such representation to enhance the credibility of the system and the fairness of its procedures.

- The employee's right jointly to select the arbitrator with the representative of the employer. This would extend as well to the selection of the mediator if mediation is involved.

- Reasonable arrangements for discovery and deposition worked out by the representatives of the parties with any disputes thereon to be resolved by the arbitrator.

- The arbitrator's authority to conduct the hearing, rule on arbitrability, evidence, post-hearing briefs, and other questions, and issue a written opinion and award consistent with the applicable rules, regulations and law. That authority would extend to the right to grant whatever relief would be available in the applicable court under the law.

- The right of the agency to overrule an award it believes to be clearly repugnant to the relevant statutes.

The letter concluded with the following:

If this proposal is acceptable, my suggestion is that the Commission do the following:

1.   Satisfy itself and the EEOC that the procedure and deferral concept is reasonable and valid.

2.   Promulgate a regulation to adopt procedures consistent with *Protocol* standards retaining the right to reject awards that are inconsistent with its announcement or the *Spielberg-Olin* standards. That could be accomplished by a statewide conference of leading employers, or by having employers develop and adopt procedures prior to the announcement.

3.   Meet with local Task Force designees to establish requirements of panel selection, of training and panel administration.

4.   Advise claimants of the mediation and arbitration alternative.

In December 1995, Chairman Duffy convened a meeting with representatives of the management and plaintiff bar to discuss elements of the procedure. Thereafter, he held a series of meetings with various interested parties and began working on the draft of a policy on the use of ADR to resolve discrimination cases filed at the MCAD.

On February 14, 1996, ten weeks after Zack sent the initial letter, Chairman Michael T. Duffy and Commissioners Dorca I. Gomez and Charles E. Walker Jr. issued Policy 96–1, Policy on Alternative Dispute Resolution.[3] It was announced at a conference held at MIT under the auspices of the Sloan School of Management. (For the full text of this document, see Appendix C.)

The Components of MCAD Policy 96–1

In its preamble, Policy 96–1 recognized the value of mediation and arbitration as a low-cost and expeditious means of bringing an equitable conclusion to the ever-growing number of complaints in discrimination cases. It also cited the requirement of voluntary selection of mediation or arbitration by both parties, and the value of ADR only "where minimum standards of quality and procedural safeguards" would make sure that "just and fair processes and outcomes" could be achieved.

The commission's practice is to offer the ADR option at the conciliation meeting—a statutorily mandated session between the parties that follows an investigation (which might take up to a year) culminating in a probable cause finding. The conciliation session lays out the options for the employer and the claimant: they can make use of mediation and arbitration to facilitate the resolution of their dispute, or turn to the traditional litigation process. The latter would take six months for a hearing before a single Commissioner, and, if appealed, another six months for a hearing before the full three-person Commission. And it is not over then; after the Commission has rendered its decision, there is always the

potential for continuing litigation between the parties in the courts
and the appeals that flow therefrom. The Commission representative points out that continued litigation and appeals are unfortunately likely, as the deep-pocket employer often seeks to pressure
the overwhelmed claimant with resolution or withdrawal.

Both parties must voluntarily agree to mediation or arbitration
after an opportunity to confer with counsel, and the Commission
will not require arbitration imposed by any predispute agreement
or any mandatory condition of employment. However, as soon as
the parties choose mediation or arbitration, the Commission sus-
pends its complaint process pending receipt of a settlement or the
arbitrator's decision.

Once the commitment to arbitration is made, the case proceeds in conformity with the MCAD procedures. They track the
Protocol with a few variations. The MCAD provides a staff attorney
in arbitrations where the claimant would otherwise proceed pro se.
That is, it encourages the parties to secure representation and offers
the claimant suggestions for representation, providing the staff
attorney only when there would otherwise be no representation.
Although there is some cost involved for the Commission, this service assures that the arbitrator will have adequate presentations to
encourage valid and unrejected awards, and thereby helps the parties and the Commission avoid litigation. In addition to the
increased satisfaction level, the service is cost-effective, as it is less
expensive than providing plaintiff representation through lengthy
litigation and appeals as MCAD's mandate requires.

The arbitrators for MCAD cases come from a demographically
diverse roster established by nomination from representative users
and approved by the MCAD. These arbitrators have undergone
both procedural and substantive training. They may be selected by
the parties or (at the parties' option) be appointed by the Commission. The qualifications for inclusion on the panel include arbitration or litigation experience or both, completion of annual
training, and familiarity with civil rights statutes and court deci-

sions. Selection for cases will depend on the statutory areas of training undertaken by the arbitrators.

The rules recognize the arbitrator's decision as final and binding if it is allowed to stand for thirty days after its filing with the Commission. During that period it can be set side by an order of two of the commissioners on the grounds that it is not in the public interest based on any of the following criteria:

- The award was procured by corruption, fraud, or other undue means.
- There was evident partiality by an arbitrator, or corruption or misconduct prejudicing either party's rights.
- The arbitrator exceeded his or her powers or refused to hear material evidence.
- The decision of the arbitrator is palpably wrong or is clearly repugnant to the purposes and policies of the Commission.

If a decision is rejected, the case is placed back to the point at which the parties elected arbitration in the commission's procedures, and then proceeds to adjudication with the arbitrator's decision admissible at a public hearing if the case is reinstated at the Commission.

The rules also introduce a procedure for what the Commission calls "non-binding arbitration." Under that procedure the parties may agree in advance to submit to nonbinding arbitration pursuant to its regular procedures, except that the party dissatisfied with the result must pay legal fees and costs of the opposing side in the arbitration before the case is reinstated, with the arbitrator's decision admissible at a public hearing if the case is reinstated at the Commission.

The policy also sets forth similar standards for mediation prior to or at any stage in the arbitration when jointly agreed. The mediation is done by a trained mediator from a comparable roster maintained by the Commission, with similar compensation provisions, and settlement agreements submitted to the MCAD for approval before a case is closed. The Commission may decline to recognize a settlement agreement and keep the case open if one of the parties was unrepresented by counsel, if the terms of the settlement are at a substantial variance with the outcomes of other cases with similar fact patterns and a reasonable explanation is lacking, or the public interest requires the Commission to keep the case open. The mediation proceedings, the positions of the parties, and the parties' offers and counteroffers made during mediation are confidential and inadmissible in any subsequent proceedings at the Commission or in court.

Selection of the Administering Agency

On February 15, 1996, Chairman Duffy published a Request for Proposals[4] addressed to administrative agencies interested in providing the ADR services. The Commission held a bidders conference on March 8, 1996, and close to a dozen potential vendors attended the session. The deadline for accepting proposals was March 29, 1996. There were three formal proposals.

Listed in the scope of services was the maintenance of a roster, investigating qualification of arbitrators and mediators, training arbitrators and mediators, annual training and evaluation, and administration of the structure. The vendor was authorized to assess fees on various parties for each component of service, including roster application fees, training fees, and administrative fees. There was also provision for evaluation procedures, which are being undertaken by a consortium headed by Thomas Kochan of the MIT Sloan School of Management. Kochan is monitoring the results achieved by the program to provide guidance to other jurisdictions seeking to learn from the Massachusetts model.

At the time, in April 1996, the AAA was considering the national adoption of its experimental "California" employment rules, which required the arbitrator to conform to the terms of the employer-promulgated arbitration agreement. At that stage the

AAA was proposing that it alone would name panel members and would restrict training to those it named to its employment panel. These positions would have precluded AAA administration of the MCAD program. On May 7, 1996, however, the AAA issued a draft announcement that it would be issuing a new set of employment rules binding arbitrators to procedures consistent with the *Protocol* and it would make the internal changes to meet the requirements of MCAD Policy 96–1.

On May 14, 1996, the MCAD met formally and unanimously voted to designate the AAA to administer the program. According to a press release on the selection, Chairman Duffy stated: "In the end we went with the AAA because of their national reputation, experience and administrative capability."

The program was operational by the end of July 1996.

The preference of claimants for mediation as a means of protecting privacy in discrimination cases is underscored by the experience of the MCAD program during its first six months of operation. Of the eleven cases accepting ADR, eight opted for mediation and three for arbitration. Five of the eleven cases were picked from the MCAD backlog awaiting hearing, one of which had been pending since 1993, and two since 1994. Five of the cases were relatively new, having been filed in 1996.

The first case arose from a claim of a thirty-three-year-old female who said she had been subjected to gender-based intimidation, humiliation, and sexual harassment at work, particularly by one supervisor. Her claims included severe psychological stress, anxiety and depression requiring medical care, loss of business reputation and respect, and loss of a significant personal relationship. She claimed damages in excess of $200,000 for emotional distress and loss of business reputation. The respondent denied that its personnel's hostile conduct, if any, was gender-based. After several mediation sessions, the case was settled with damages paid, but with the parties agreeing to keep the terms confidential. In exit interviews both parties said they would use the system again. The employer is considering the program on all cases where charges have been filed and will use the process as an internal learning and educational tool.

The second case involved a racial discrimination charge by a thirty-one-year-old male of Jamaican descent, who filed against a large construction firm when he was laid off after two months of work. He claimed $40,000 in lost wages, and $750,000 for emotional distress. The employer claimed he was laid off for poor performance. No offers of settlement were made at the mediation and the case was set for public hearing.

Another case involved an employee grieving through his union against a town while also filing a claim with the MCAD. The MCAD and the parties agreed to combine the two cases before a mutually agreed-upon arbitrator. The charges were consolidated with the collective bargaining case and is pending a hearing.

A fourth case involved a claim filed by a twenty-three-year-old female working in an automotive center, and included liability, lost wages, and severe emotional distress totaling $1,000,000 because of sexual harassment, sexual assaults, comments, and lewd graffiti creating a hostile environment. The respondent denied the claims and stated the claimant never reported or objected to any alleged harassment though knowing of company policy against such wrongdoing, and pointed out that the claimant had voluntarily resigned and gone to work for a competitor at a higher pay rate. It also noted that medical records from her therapist did not substantiate any emotional problems. She also had a history of suing for personal injury and had sufficient experience in the court system to know about complaint filing. The case settled at mediation within twenty-four hours after agreement to mediate.

Summary

The choice of Massachusetts for the initial exploration of a state program was in a sense fortuitous. But the rapid development of an operational program was the result of innovation, foresight, and hard work on the part of the MCAD and particularly Chairman Duffy. The MCAD experience is providing a model for other jurisdictions to extend the use of the *Protocol* to resolve discrimination claims expeditiously. The enthusiasm of the MCAD Chairman and staff, along with the professional evaluation being undertaken under the leadership of the MIT Sloan School of Management, are providing guidance to other jurisdictions seeking to expand the application of ADR to discrimination law.

Chapter Nine

The Future of Employment Law Dispute Resolution

The characteristics of American workplaces, the inaccessibility of statutory protections for many workers with or without collective bargaining agreements, and the Supreme Court's endorsement of arbitration have created a new opportunity for protecting workers' statutory rights through mediation and arbitration. The growing support for ADR systems, coupled with some early experiments that assure due process protections, demonstrate the potential for such voluntary dispute resolution through private workplace procedures and through government agencies encouraging their adoption.

At the same time, there is growing frustration with the consequences of agency budget restraints, reduced governmental enforcement, increasing court delays, rising costs of legal representation, and reduced access to effective public regulatory protections. The development of due process protections in employment disputes opens the door to expanded use of such procedures in a variety of conflicts as the most effective means of assuring citizen recourse to otherwise unattainable statutory protections. The success of efforts in the employment field may indeed be a call for expanding the processes of mediation and arbitration to a much broader range of citizen efforts to achieve statutory protections.

This chapter is divided into three sections. The first gives an overall picture of the American workplace. The second discusses the growing resort to ADR generally, and the third assesses the role of various constituencies in the future of employment law dispute resolution.

The American Workplace

To appreciate the complexity and limitations of traditional statutory regulation, it is essential to understand the diversity of American workplaces, the characteristics of the workforce, and the turbulence in the labor market. Civilian employment in the United States in 1995 approximated 125 million, 53.9 percent male and 46.1 percent female. Another 7.4 million persons were unemployed and seeking employment.

Civilian employment included 8.9 million self-employed in nonagricultural industries, excluded from many employment statutes and regulations. Nineteen percent of the aggregate civilian employed reported they worked part time rather than full time. There were more than six million different civilian workplaces.

These workplaces are managed by firms with practices and outcomes for workers that differ widely, depending to great extent on the number of employees. At one extreme, 5.7 million workers are employed in establishments with under five employees, and 13.4 million are in establishments with under ten employees. At the other end of the size spectrum, 11.3 million workers are employed in establishments with over a thousand employees.

Since large firms often have many establishments—stores, plants, locations—the distribution by *firm* size shows a greater degree of concentration. Firms with over a thousand employees employ 35.2 percent of the workforce, compared with 12.2 percent employed by firms with under ten employees.[1]

Employment law statutes often have exclusions by the size of the enterprise, measured by the number of employees or the dollar-volume of business, as well as an agriculture exemption. As noted earlier, in the case of the OSHA injury and illness log, the threshold level is ten employees; the threshold for the Family and Medical Leave Act is fifty employees, and in the case of the Workers Adjustment and Retraining Notification Act the figure is a hundred. In general, firms that do not meet a $500,000 test of annual business are excluded from the Fair Labor Standards Act.[2]

Another feature of the American workplace that affects statutory rights is the widespread and continual creation and destruction of firms, establishments, and jobs. "Existing plants expand or contrast, new plants start up, and old plants shut down. . . . Large-scale job creation and destruction turn out to be pervasive among countries, regions, industries, and various types of plants and firms."[3] The magnitude of these changes in manufacturing is reflected in the fact that over a typical twelve-month period about 10 percent of jobs disappear and a comparable number of new manufacturing jobs open up at different locations. Smaller manufacturing firms and plants exhibit sharply higher gross job creation rates but not higher net creation rates. Large, mature plants and firms account for most newly created—and newly destroyed—manufacturing jobs.[4]

In a more general and analytical sense, each workplace is distinctive, defined by its technology, its product and labor markets, and its community and governmental regulatory setting or environment.[5] A complex of detailed rules of the workplace—governing compensation and benefits, hours, work standards including discipline and safety—develop in this context, constructed either by management alone or through the processes of collective bargaining with a labor organization. The technical context of workplaces and their related rules varies: there are fixed workplaces as in a manufacturing plant, variable locations as with airplane flight crews and traveling salespersons, and workplaces including residences as with jobs on a vessel or in a logging camp; there are also variations in the size of the work group, the diverse dimensions of job content, and the required hours of operations as in continuous industry. The nature and quality of product and labor markets influence the degree of competition impinging on the workplace, including international competition, and the community influences the ethnic, racial, and educational levels of available workers. Managements—working alone or with labor organizations—have some degrees of freedom as to the forms of internal organization at the workplace and qualities of the relationships established, such as in employee involvement programs and teams, but these contexts tend to prescribe narrow limits as to the substantive rules and policies adopted at each workplace. In any event, the range of work rules vary widely among these diverse workplaces.

In sum, the American workplace has become a central institution in our society.[6] A higher proportion of the population than ever before is in the workplace, as women have taken jobs to support their families as principal breadwinners or as part of dual-earner households. Workplaces reflect the racial and ethnic diversity of communities more than any other institution. The workplace distributes earned income to most of the population, and in contrast with many other advanced countries, the United States relies on private decision making in the workplace to furnish a disparate range of benefits, most notably health insurance and paid vacations.

The workplace is a centerpiece of the nation's economic performance and of its concern with productivity, quality, and competitiveness. The workplace is also the locus of vital training of the workforce and even of considerable formal education programs, illustrated by instruction in math, language, and basic skills, apprenticeship, military programs, interns and residents in the medical profession, and executive training. Training in health and safety, quality, and problem solving are critical for the workplace to fulfill both its social and economic roles. Moreover, new forms of work organization have been emerging, including employee involvement, teams, work at home, new work hours and new legal forms, changing traditional relationships among workers and supervisors as well as among workers themselves, and even with customers.

It is into this setting that we must place the growing federal and state regulation of the workplace. The workplace becomes the focus of concern of citizens, where they spend much of their time, and where conditions of work impinge directly on their personal lives. Citizens seek a role for government to protect and enhance their workaday experience. Starting in the early 1900s with concern over accidents, a vastly expanded array of government standards has been required of workplaces by the political process. Through Republican and Democratic administrations alike over the years, this complex of statutes and their regulations has greatly expanded, with different administrative agencies and procedures for adjudication and enforcement, even in the same department of the federal government.

There appears to be wide public support for the social objectives and purposes of much of this legislation, particularly with an increased proportion of the population in the civilian workforce (from 58.8 percent in 1962 to 66.6 percent in 1995). But there is widespread dissatisfaction with the prevailing process of issuing regulations, and the prescribed procedures for their adjudication in individual cases, as many employees are unable to achieve their statutory rights. In some areas, as in the Wage and Hour statute in the women's clothing industry, there is even widespread noncompliance. Given the vast diversity of workplaces and regulations, it seems useful to develop alternative voluntary means to adjudicate differences and disputes over employment law.

The complexities of the American workplace, the range of employment options, the heterogeneity of the workforce, the scope of enacted protective legislation, and the variations in statutory coverage demonstrate the futility of expecting general legislation and litigation to achieve full worker protection. One size does not fit all. It is becoming increasingly clear as the economy grows, as the coverage and quantity of regulatory legislation grows, and as the public seeks to restrict the size and role of government, that a new approach toward decentralized enforcement of statutory employment rights is required—if not long overdue.

The Growing Resort to ADR

Beyond these characteristics of the American workplace that are congenial to decentralized dispute resolution, the prospects of mediation and arbitration in the adjudication of employment law disputes are enhanced by their growing use in dispute resolution generally, as well as in the legal system outside of employment law.

Workplace participants are not isolated from the influences impinging on all parties in this litigious society. Moreover, a number of statutes, including the Administrative Dispute Resolution Act (1990) and its 1996 replacement, have explicitly authorized and sought to encourage the use of ADR in the adjudication of disputes arising under statutes.

A few illustrations of these wider and recent developments may be cited. As noted in Chapter Seven, President Clinton has issued an executive order on civil justice reform.[7] That order states in part:

> And to improve access to justice for all persons who wish to avail themselves of court and administrative adjudicatory tribunals to resolve disputes, to facilitate the just and efficient resolution of civil claims involving the United States Government . . . and to provide a model for similar reforms of litigation practices in the private sector and in various states, it is hereby ordered as follows:
>
> Section 1, (c)(1) Whenever feasible claims should be resolved through informal discussions, negotiations, and settlements rather than through utilization of any court proceedings. Where the benefits of Alternative Dispute Resolution (ADR) may be derived, and after consultation with the agency referring the matter, litigation counsel should suggest the use of an appropriate ADR technique to the practice.
>
> (c)(3) To facilitate broader and effective use of informal and formal ADR methods, litigation counsel should be trained in ADR techniques.

Section 3 of the order explicitly requires agencies formulating proposed legislation and regulations to make every reasonable effort to ensure "whether private arbitration and other forms of private dispute resolution are appropriate . . . subject to constitutional requirements."[8] Thus, federal agencies and their administrators are instructed to develop and to use ADR methods, including mediation and final and binding arbitration, in the civil justice system in appropriate cases.

Another illustration is provided by Department of Defense Directive 5145.4, "Alternative Dispute Resolution," issued on April 22, 1996. This directive establishes a framework for encouraging and expanding the use of ADR within the Defense Department.[9] The directive envisions wide application of ADR: "Every dispute, regardless of subject matter is a potential for ADR."

Between 1987 and 1994, the Armed Services Board of Contract Appeals found that "ADR was successful in more than 90 percent of the instances in which it had been used." A judge of the Armed Services Board of Contract Appeals reported to the ABA Section of Public Contract Law on May 2, 1996, that "A party should not expect a reward for merely participating in the ADR process. Many believe there is a tendency for the arbitrator to 'split the baby', but in my experience this does not occur. Meritless claims will not fare better in ADR."

Brief mention is appropriate of Vice President Gore's report, *Creating a Government that Works Better and Costs Less*, which includes two specific recommendations directed to the Labor Department:[10] "DOL 03 Expand Negotiated Rulemaking and Improve Up-Front Teamwork on Regulations" and "DOL 04 Expand the Use of Alternative Dispute Resolution by the Department of Labor." Despite these admonitions, as noted in Chapter Seven, Labor Department regulators have been very lethargic about moving in this direction. But White House policies should be helpful in the long term, along with the legislation of 1990 and 1996, in setting a climate to encourage these methods of developing regulations and their adjudication—and in eroding bureaucratic opposition.

In the field of environmental regulation, prior to 1993 the resort to negotiated rulemaking and ADR methods of adjudication received greater attention than in employment law. These developments were encouraged by the attitudes of the Environmental Protection Agency regulators, the Department of Energy, environmental groups, business interests, and by several skillful neutrals—including Philip A. Harter, a leader working with the

Administrative Law Conference in the advocacy and practice of ADR,[11] and Gerald W. Cormick. One more recent illustration is the Joint Cooperative Council for Hanford Disputes, which seeks to address whistleblowing and other concerns of employees at the Hanford, Washington site.[12]

In the environmental field, Resolve, Inc.—with its Center for Environmental Dispute Resolution and its publication, *Resolve*—provides information about environmental dispute resolution approaches. By 1984 there were about two hundred cases in which alternate dispute resolution methods had been undertaken,[13] and by the mid–1990s it is reported there were at least an additional thousand cases.[14]

Another instance of a formal organization designed to reduce litigation and to promote ADR methods in a sector is DART, the construction industry Dispute Avoidance and Resolution Task Force.[15] That conglomerate sector has been plagued by a variety of business disputes involving owners, architects, engineers and professional societies, developers, general contractors and specialty contractors, and insurers on private and public sector projects, apart from labor-management disputes under collective bargaining. The end result of this conflict, DART emphasizes, is lower productivity, lower quality, higher costs, lower profits, and a pervasive feeling of frustration and genuine lack of satisfaction and accomplishment. The *Business Roundtable* referred to the "adversarial dance" between participants as creating a "constant state of confrontation" between parties to a contract. The *Engineering News-Record* deplored the "awful litigious nature of the industry" and pointed out that much of this litigation is bred by the "unabashed risk-shifting which is flourishing in the writing of construction contracts." Participants with economic power try to "stick it to the other guy."

DART was organized in 1991 by a range of industry representatives, including lawyers, with the cooperation of the AAA. Its statements outline three reasons for its formation: the construction industry's frustration with the adversarial climate of recent years, general frustration with the court system as a way of resolving disputes, and the development of a variety of ADR methods.[16] The organization aims to secure a predispute pledge from all parties to a project to participate in partnering, team building, and dispute resolution procedures as long as the project lasts.

DART developed a series of seminars for the various constituencies in the industry, and in 1993 began a program of awards to parties and to projects that adopted dispute resolution procedures that were both innovative and effective.[17] In 1996, it issued "The Dart Declaration of Principles" to be signed by each party participating in a project as an expression of a "serious and good faith desire to cooperatively achieve solutions to problems and resolution of claims and disputes in a manner which will avoid engaging in formal dispute resolution procedures."

Brief mention may also be made of other developments affecting the gradual spread of methods of dispute resolution outside administrative tribunals and the courts. A standard reference work has appeared for applying ADR techniques to disputes involving financial institutions.[18] Some disputes may primarily involve individuals rather than organizations. Domestic relations advocacy, which seeks various forms of settlement outside the courts or agreements that a court ratifies, is an illustration.[19] The field of landlord-tenant relations has cases that are of a similar nature in which informal procedures have emerged.

Finally, the considerable growth in recent years of negotiations programs in law schools, business schools, and public policy education programs may be expected to influence a younger generation of executives and practitioners, in appropriate cases, to practice what they have been taught.

The work of the AAA, J.A.M.S./Endispute, the Society of Professionals in Dispute Resolution, the ACLU, and the training role in mediation of the FMCS for the staffs of government agencies also need to be mentioned. Organizations in particular sectors or concerned with special issues are also arising, as has been noted, to make a contribution to dispute resolution through ADR methods.

The developments and tendencies briefly sketched in this section are a part of a larger setting in which issues of employment law adjudication arise. This climate is encouraging resort to mediation and arbitration in employment law disputes.

Mediation and Arbitration: The Matrix of Policies and Institutions

The major institutional players in employment law will need several adaptations and arrangements to provide due process resolution of disputes for the wide spectrum of workers and workplaces in the country today. These constituencies include management organizations; regulatory agencies; labor, civil rights, women's and various human rights organizations; the legislatures; the courts; neutral mediators and arbitrators; and the agencies that designate the neutrals. Each of these groups is a potential beneficiary from an expansion in voluntary adjudication of employment law disputes. One also needs to recognize the role in research, evaluation, and advocacy exercised by members of various professional associations with interests in the labor market.

The gradual development of voluntary dispute resolution in employment law requires a matrix of consistent arrangements and policies within and among these institutions. The administrative agencies will retain substantial authority, and that authority places on them a large and continuing responsibility both for the voluntary arrangements and for their own role and that of the courts in the adjudication of employment law. As has been noted earlier, not all disputes are appropriate for ADR. Some cases involve class actions and others raise possible questions of criminal law; some have potential for policy precedents and for continuing legislative oversight, and still others may require remedies for patterns of practice that only an administrative agency and the courts should resolve. In some disputes, so many parties may care to be involved that conventional processes are actually more efficient than ADR. Further, there are complex cases that involve a number of agencies and procedures in a single episode, as in the case of the termination of an employee that may raise possible concerns under the OSHA, the Age Discrimination in Employment Act, the Americans with Disabilities Act, and other employment laws. Moreover, for a long time and likely in the long term, despite the prospects of lower costs and faster decisions, many individual parties will prefer traditional adjudication.

It will take a long time to train the numerous administrative staffs within government agencies in the arts of mediation and arbitration, or to replace the traditional and legalistic generation of civil servants who follow an ideology of litigation with a new generation attuned to the advantages of ADR. It will take a considerable period to establish a system of significant size in the private adjudication of public law disputes. There will be many skirmishes and battles within and among these organizations.

Management Organizations

Management includes private businesses, nonprofit organizations, and government agencies as employers. They are all, in varying degrees and ways, subject to the provisions of employment statutes and regulations.[20]

American jurisprudence and practice draws a complex distinction between employees eligible for union organization in a collective bargaining unit and managers, supervisors, and exempt employees who are not eligible for union organization. Both categories of employees may be involved in disputes over employment law issues.

Many management organizations, particularly larger ones, have developed internal and informal procedures to resolve all manner of disputes.[21] In nonunion settings, various complaint procedures or open-door policies have been defined; a number of these plans include a designated professional, an ombudsperson, responsible for handling and seeking resolution of employee complaints as they arise.[22] In union settings, the contractual grievance procedure has often become more mediatory and informal. (See Chapter Six.)

In a nonunion setting, the design of the internal dispute resolution plan requires considerable care, as some plans may be found to violate Section 8(a)(2) of the LMRA (which concerns employer-dominated labor organizations). The establishment of an ombudsperson alone to resolve disputes does not appear to violate the statute. The general counsel of the NLRB dismissed charges against a company that had established such an office on the grounds that the ombudsperson did not involve employee participation.[23] In this case the internal ombudsperson was to explain company policies and procedures, advise on alternative courses of action, refer to appropriate contacts, arrange meetings, mediate the dispute, follow up on conflict resolutions, recommend changes to management, and the like. But an employee committee or organization was not involved.

But there are other cases in which the NLRB has found management-sponsored grievance committees of employees to be unlawfully dominated by the employer. That is, the NLRB has held, the "committee is not capable of action independent of the employer, and is prohibited."[24]

If permissible internal procedures are unable to resolve a dispute over employment law between a management organization and an employee, the option of a voluntary referral of the dispute to an appropriate outside procedure (other than the government agency or to the courts) for mediation and final and binding settlement is the present recommendation. The requisite condition is the option for voluntary referral to a process and to neutrals who provide due process by the standards defined in detail in Chapter Six. These standards are likely to prove essential if an administrative agency is to defer to arbitration and the courts are to support such referral. The need for deferral is necessary in union and nonunion workplaces alike, and among categories of employees ordinarily ineligible for labor organization, if an integrated system of private resolution of employment law disputes is to be established.

Business and labor organizations and the various administrative agencies need to approach consensus with regard to these standards of due process, the requisite training of neutrals, and a procedure for the selection of neutrals in individual cases. There is need for congruence between systems of dispute resolution established or recognized by business under collective bargaining agreements and those established or recognized by the several government agencies, and eventually by the courts.

The Task Force on Excellence in State and Local Government reports that there appears to be more receptivity and fewer barriers to ADR methods in resolving law disputes in state and local government than in the private sector.[25] Many private sector employers have sought to require such arbitration as a condition of employment; public managers under civil service statutes and pervasive political processes are less able and less interested in making arbitration a condition of employment. Public managers appear more willing than private employees to propose dispute resolution programs that meet the tests of due process. That Task Force recommended a set of standards for ADR building on those of the Commission and the *Protocol*. "The Task Force encourages the voluntary development of such systems and urges national employer, labor and rights groups to assist local parties in developing such systems."[26] Both the Commission and the Task Force recommended strongly against preemployment or predispute commitments to ADR.

Regulatory Agencies

For ADR to develop with the support of regulatory agencies in employment law, at least three significant changes need to be introduced. First, a few experimental programs of voluntary mediation and arbitration need to be identified by regulatory agencies with specified standards of due process, as well as the designation of types of cases excluded from the voluntary process. In these experimental programs, voluntary mediation and arbitration should be proffered after an agency has become aware of a possible violation, such as after a finding of probable cause. A number of such experiments in federal and state agencies are already under way, such as those in the Massachusetts Commission Against Discrimination, the mediation program of the EEOC, the pilot programs proposed for comment in the Labor Department, and the "carve out" programs in workers' compensation in some states. (Chapters Seven and Eight describe these programs in some detail.) The experience under these and other programs should be carefully monitored and dispassionately evaluated for more general application.

Second, arrangements need to be made for selection and training of outside mediators and arbitrators. This training needs to cover both the substance of the statutes and regulations administered by the agency and the principles and techniques of dispute resolution.

Third, the legal and investigatory staffs of the agencies require training, as the FMCS is providing, in ADR methods and procedures. Voluntary adjudicatory processes are enhanced as the agencies also seek to use the method of negotiated rulemaking in approaching new regulations or in reviewing long-standing rules that may require revision.

The design of the ADR systems in these pilot programs will benefit from interactions with labor and management representatives affected by the statutory provisions. It will also be useful to obtain comments from some experienced neutrals and members of the bar.

In the general dissatisfaction with the procedures agencies and the courts currently use to resolve disputes over employment law, all parties need to be alert to the diversified opportunities for responsible innovation that have been presenting themselves—some promising and others of dubious value—in the ferment over alternative procedures. In Massachusetts, for instance, the outside section of the 1997 budget provides for the arbitration of claims before the Civil Service Commission and complaints issued by the Labor Relations Commission following the filing of charges. Arbitrators would be selected under procedures of the AAA or the Massachusetts Board of Conciliation and Arbitration.[27] Such opportunities need to be professionally addressed within the framework presented in this volume. The congruence of procedures developed by management organizations and by regulatory agencies is important to the emergence of a total matrix of private adjudication of employment law disputes.

Labor Organizations

The broadening of the grievance procedures in workplaces governed by collective bargaining agreements will provide union members, and those represented by unions, an added and enhanced service. Inasmuch as the collective agreement in *Alexander* v. *Gardner-Denver* did not specifically authorize the arbitrator to make a statutory interpretation, such explicit authorization might be supported by the courts today. This direction would be encouraged by writing into collective bargaining agreements the statutory rights to which employees are entitled and authorizing the arbitrator to rule on grievances alleging statutory violations with remedies comparable to those established by law.

The Commission on the Future of Worker-Management Relations stated that it believes there is considerable scope for innovation in these systems. "For example, unions, professional associations, and other worker advocacy groups may wish to market their services in representing individuals in these processes and providing technical advice and services in the design and oversight of these systems."[28] A role in the resolution of disputes over employment law would provide a new function for labor organizations under collective agreements as well as assisting workers without representation. It would also require that union representatives receive additional training in statutory rights and the representation of workers in employment law disputes.[29]

Neutral Mediators and Arbitrators

There is likely to be a growing market for professional mediators and arbitrators trained and experienced in employment law dispute resolution. The groups can be drawn from arbitrators under collective bargaining agreements and from those experienced with employment law regimes as inspectors, investigators, litigators, and administrators. But each group will need significant additional training in the part of the ideal combined background that its members lack. Present arbitrators require background in the statutes and regulations, while those with agency, labor, or management background in the field need the training of neutral mediators and arbitrators. ADR in employment law requires the development of a new specialized profession. The existing neutrals and their professional associations also have a role in assisting in the recruitment and training of this specialized profession of neutrals.

The neutrals as well as the advocates should promptly address the development of a code of ethics or a code of professional responsibility to protect the credibility of employment arbitration procedures by assuring that there is full disclosure of any challengeable relationship between the neutrals and the parties and their representatives, to assure that the arbitrators do not undertake such cases without adequate qualification, and to assure adherence to due process standards. Such a code has enhanced the acceptability of union-management arbitration and will contribute to the respect accorded employment arbitration.

Legislatures

The development of a private sector adjudication of employment law disputes eventually requires the acceptance or adoption by the legislature or the courts of a set of standards for due process, in one pronouncement or on a case-by-case basis, ideally along the lines proposed in Chapter Four and articulated by the Commission on the Future of Worker-Management Relations, the State and Local Government Task Force, and the *Protocol*. The Commission, the task force, and the NAA would also specify as a standard that a dispute resolution plan cannot be made a condition of employment when it requires a waiver of access to a judicial or administrative forum for statutory rights. Rather, it should be evoked voluntarily after a dispute has arisen.

Courts

Some modification or clarification of *Alexander* v. *Gardner-Denver* (1974) and *Gilmer* v. *Interstate/Johnson Lane Corp*. (1991) are required for an effective system of private dispute resolution of employment law disputes. If voluntary arbitration of employment law disputes were to be extended to nonunion workplaces and to categories of employees not ordinarily eligible for representation, then it would not be a large step to modify *Alexander* and to extend such voluntary arbitration to employees governed by a collective bargaining agreement and a grievance procedure, provided statutory rights were incorporated in the agreement, of course, with suitably trained arbitrators and with standards of due process.

Several aspects of *Gilmer* need attention. The case upheld the commitment to arbitration made as a condition of employment. There is widespread hostility to this view for employment generally (without regard to the brokerage industry); women's organizations, civil rights groups, labor organizations, the NAA, the EEOC, and the NLRB—and many others—are opposed on grounds of fairness and the realities of the labor market. This issue might be resolved in defining the standards for due process arbitration.

Another aspect of *Gilmer* is that the decision explicitly left open the larger issue of the specification of standards for arbitration. That opening permits the development of a set of safeguards and standards of due process by the courts along the lines presented in the *Protocol* and in Chapter Six. The Court should bar the enforcement of employer-promulgated arbitration systems that deny employees basic due process protections—and it should define the essential elements of due process standards. Further, there is need to clarify the scope of the Federal Arbitration Act as it relates to employment statutes and the securities industry. Finally, the courts should reserve to themselves or the administrative agencies the right to review whether arbitration decisions meet an appropriate standard of deferral, such as *Spielberg-Olin*.

Agencies Designating Neutrals

The acceptability of mediation and arbitration of statutory disputes is enhanced by the essential role of the designating agencies such as J.A.M.S./Endispute and the AAA. Both agencies have given legitimacy to the *Protocol* by integrating its components into their current rules. At the same time, they have enhanced their own credibility by taking the position that they will only administer cases pursuant to their new rules. The result of their venture has been to isolate employers who had exploited the good names of the designating agencies by claiming that agency administration of questionable employer-created programs made them valid and fair. Once the agencies departed from the position that they would enforce any employer-promulgated arbitration agreement, announcing they would henceforth enforce only those that met standards of due process, they forced into open scrutiny those employer programs that do not use these agencies because the price of fairness may be too dear. The designating agencies have thus given enhanced credibility to the whole structure of statutory arbitration.

The FMCS should adopt the same standards as the other major appointing agencies in employment law cases under employer-promulgated programs, whether panels are named or appointments made under its statutory authority or in response to a request for a panel or the appointment of an arbitrator pursuant to a request under the Freedom of Information Act.[30]

The agencies that designate neutrals have the further responsibility to develop lists of mediators and arbitrators with experience in these dispute resolution processes and knowledgeable in various specialties of employment law. They have a major role, with professional associations and agencies, in the training of neutrals in these fields and expanding the cadre of acceptable mediators and arbitrators in employment law disputes.

Summary

This volume constitutes a challenge to the constituencies involved in employment law disputes to promulgate and administer voluntary systems of dispute resolution that meet the standards of fairness and due process. The courts have given a green light to arbitration instead of litigation. The administrative agencies seek relief from backlogs. Managements seek relief from litigation. Workers in union and nonunion settings seek less expensive and quicker resolution of their claims for rights and protections provided by statutes and agency regulations.

Over the next decade or so, the institutional players identified here have the capacity to develop and place into effect a matrix of policies and procedures to establish a congruent and voluntary system of mediation and arbitration in employment law disputes. This system would not govern all cases of disputes, by any means, but it would constitute a significant option providing more rapid and less expensive decisions with roughly equivalent results—and many more resolutions—than provided by the present administrative agencies and the courts.

The widespread acceptance of due process procedures for employment law disputes, as developed in this volume, would do much to extend such principles to other litigious fields in this society. As noted in the Preface, mediation and arbitration implemented in accordance with due process procedures can do much to resolve statutory and regulatory disputes in the fields of health care, the environment, insurance, family protection, and other areas of societal concern. Resolution of workplace disputes is only the first step in bringing more justice to more people through a fair, affordable, and expeditious procedure for conflict resolution.

Appendix A

List of Acronyms

The following are designated by acronyms throughout the book. The first time an item is introduced, the acronym follows in parentheses.

- Alternative Dispute Resolution (ADR)
- American Arbitration Association (AAA)
- American Bar Association (ABA)
- American Civil Liberties Union (ACLU)
- Equal Employment Opportunity Commission (EEOC)
- Federal Mediation and Conciliation Service (FMCS)
- Judicial Arbitration and Mediation Services/Endispute (J.A.M.S./Endispute)
- Labor-Management Relations Act (LMRA)
- National Labor Relations Board (NLRB)
- Occupational Safety and Health Act (OSHA)
- Due Process Protocol for Mediation and Arbitration of Statutory Disputes Arising out of the Employment Relationship (the *Protocol*)
- Securities Exchange Commission (SEC)

The following items are designated by acronyms in a chapter if they appear in that chapter more than twice. As above, the acronym is in parentheses at first mention.

- Administrative Conference of the United States (ACUS)
- Age Discrimination in Employment Act (ADEA)

- Construction Industry Dispute Avoidance and Resolution Task Force (DART)
- Massachusetts Commission Against Discrimination (MCAD)
- National Academy of Arbitrators (NAA)

Appendix B

The Protocol

Due Process Protocol for Mediation and Arbitration of Statutory Disputes Arising Out of the Employment Relationship

The following protocol is offered by the undersigned individuals, members of the Task Force on Alternative Dispute Resolution in Employment, as a means of providing due process in the resolution by mediation and binding arbitration of employment disputes involving statutory rights. The signatories were designated by their respective organizations, but the protocol reflects their personal views and should not be construed as representing the policy of the designating organizations.

Genesis

This Task Force was created by individuals from diverse organizations involved in labor and employment law to examine questions of due process arising out of the use of mediation and arbitration for resolving employment disputes. In this protocol we confine ourselves to statutory disputes.

The members of the Task Force felt that mediation and arbitration of statutory disputes conducted under proper due process safeguards should be encouraged in order to provide expeditious, accessible, inexpensive and fair private enforcement of statutory employment disputes for the 100,000,000 members of the workforce who might not otherwise have ready, effective access to administrative or judicial relief. They also hope that such a system will serve to reduce the delays which now arise out of the huge backlog of cases pending before administrative agencies and courts and that it will help forestall an even greater number of such cases.

A. *Pre or Post Dispute Arbitration*

The Task Force recognizes the dilemma inherent in the timing of an agreement to mediate and/or arbitrate statutory disputes. It did not achieve consensus on this difficult issue. The views in this spectrum are set forth randomly, as follows:

- *Employers should be able to create mediation and/or arbitration systems to resolve statutory claims, but any agreement to mediate and/or arbitrate disputes should be informed, voluntary, and not a condition of initial or continued employment.*

- *Employers should have the right to insist on an agreement to mediate and/or arbitrate statutory disputes as a condition of initial or continued employment. Postponing such an agreement until a dispute actually arises, when there will likely exist a stronger predisposition to litigate, will result in very few agreements to mediate and/or arbitrate, thus negating the likelihood of effectively utilizing alternative dispute resolution and overcoming the problems of administrative and judicial delays which now plague the system.*

- *Employees should not be permitted to waive their right to judicial relief of statutory claims arising out of the employment relationship for any reason.*

- *Employers should be able to create mediation and/or arbitration systems to resolve statutory claims, but the decision to mediate and/or arbitrate individual cases should not be made until after the dispute arises.*

The Task Force takes no position on the timing of agreements to mediate and/or arbitrate statutory employment disputes, though it agrees that such agreements be knowingly made. The focus of this protocol is on standards of exemplary due process.

B. *Right of Representation*

1. *Choice of Representative.* Employees considering the use of or, in fact, utilizing mediation and/or arbitration procedures should have the right to be represented by a spokesperson of their own choosing. The mediation and arbitration procedure should so specify and should include reference to institutions which might offer assistance, such as bar associations, legal service associations, civil rights organizations, trade unions, etc.

2. *Fees for Representation.* The amount and method of payment for representation should be determined between the claimant and the representative. We recommend, however, a number of existing systems which provide employer reimbursement of at least a portion of the employee's attorney fees, especially for lower paid employees. The arbitrator should have the authority to provide for fee reimbursement, in whole or in part, as part of the remedy in accordance with applicable law or in the interests of justice.

3. *Access to Information.* One of the advantages of arbitration is that there is usually less time and money spent in pre-trial discovery. Adequate but limited pre-trial discovery is to be encouraged and employees should have access to all information reasonably relevant to mediation and/or arbitration of their claims. The employees' representative should also have reasonable pre-hearing and hearing access to all such information and documentation.

Necessary pre-hearing depositions consistent with the expedited nature of arbitration should be available. We also recommend that prior to selection of an arbitrator, each side should be provided with the names, addresses and phone numbers of the representatives of the parties in that arbitrator's six most recent cases to aid them in selection.

C. *Mediator and Arbitrator Qualification*

1. *Roster Membership.* Mediators and arbitrators selected for such cases should have skill in the conduct of hearings, knowledge of the statutory issues at stake in the dispute, and familiarity with the workplace and employment environment. The roster of available mediators and arbitrators should be established on a non-discriminatory basis, diverse by gender, ethnicity, background, experience, etc. to satisfy the parties that their interest and objectives will be respected and fully considered.

Our recommendation is for selection of impartial arbitrators and mediators. We recognize the right of employers and employees to jointly select as mediator and/or arbitrator one in whom both parties have requisite trust, even though not possessing the qualifications here recommended, as most promising to bring finality and to withstand judicial scrutiny. The existing cadre of labor and employment mediators and arbitrators, some lawyers, some not, although skilled in conducting hearings and familiar with the employment milieu is unlikely, without special training, to consistently possess knowledge of the statutory environment in which these disputes arise and of the characteristics of the non-union workplace.

There is a manifest need for mediators and arbitrators with expertise in statutory requirements in the employment field who may, without special training, lack experience in the employment area and in the conduct of arbitration hearings and mediation sessions.

Reexamination of rostering eligibility by designating agencies, such as the American Arbitration Association, may permit the expedited inclusion in the pool of this most valuable source of expertise.

The roster of arbitrators and mediators should contain representatives with all such skills in order to meet the diverse needs of this caseload.

Regardless of their prior experience, mediators and arbitrators on the roster must be independent of bias toward either party. They should reject cases if they believe the procedure lacks requisite due process.

2. *Training.* The creation of a roster containing the foregoing qualifications dictates the development of a training program to educate existing and potential labor and employment mediators and arbitrators as to the statutes, including substantive, procedural and remedial issues to be confronted and to train experts in the statutes as to employer procedures governing the employment relationship as well as due process and fairness in the conduct and control of arbitration hearings and mediation sessions.

Training in the statutory issues should be provided by the government agencies, bar associations, academic institutions, etc., administered perhaps by the designating agency, such as the AAA, at various locations throughout the country. Such training should be updated periodically and be required of all mediators and arbitrators. Training in the conduct of mediation and arbitration could be provided by a mentoring program with experienced panelists.

Successful completion of such training would be reflected in the résumés or panel cards of the arbitrators supplied to the parties for their selection process.

3. *Panel Selection.* Upon request of the parties, the designating agency should utilize a list procedure such as

that of the AAA or select a panel composed of an odd number of mediators and arbitrators from its roster or pool. The panel cards for such individuals should be submitted to the parties for their perusal prior to alternate striking of the names on the list, resulting in the designation of the remaining mediator and/or arbitrator.

The selection process could empower the designating agency to appoint a mediator and/or arbitrator if the striking procedure is unacceptable or unsuccessful. As noted above, subject to the consent of the parties, the designating agency should provide the names of the parties and their representatives in recent cases decided by the listed arbitrators.

4. *Conflicts of Interest.* The mediator and arbitrator for a case has a duty to disclose any relationship which might reasonably constitute or be perceived as a conflict of interest. The designated mediator and/or arbitrator should be required to sign an oath provided by the designating agency, if any, affirming the absence of such present or preexisting ties.

5. *Authority of the Arbitrator.* The arbitrator should be bound by applicable agreements, statutes, regulations and rules of procedure of the designating agency, including the authority to determine the time and place of the hearing, permit reasonable discovery, issue subpoenas, decide arbitrability issues, preserve order and privacy in the hearings, rule on evidentiary matters, determine the close of the hearing and procedures for post-hearing submissions, and issue an award resolving the submitted dispute.

The arbitrator should be empowered to award whatever relief would be available in court under the law. The arbitrator should issue an opinion and award setting forth a summary of the issues, including the type(s) of dispute(s), the damages and/or other relief requested and awarded, a statement of any other issues resolved, and a statement regarding the disposition of any statutory claim(s).

6. *Compensation of the Mediator and Arbitrator.* Impartiality is best assured by the parties sharing the fees and expenses of the mediator and arbitrator. In cases where the economic condition of a party does not permit equal sharing, the parties should make mutually acceptable arrangements to achieve that goal if at all possible. In the absence of such agreement, the arbitrator should determine allocation of fees. The designating agency, by negotiating the parties' share of costs and collecting such fees, might be able to reduce the bias potential of disparate contributions by forwarding payment to the mediator and/or arbitrator without disclosing the parties' share therein.

D. *Scope of Review*

The arbitrator's award should be final and binding and the scope of review should be limited.

Dated: May 9, 1995

Christopher A. Barecca, Co-Chair
Partner, Paul, Hastings, Janofsky & Walker
Representative, Council of Labor and Employment Section, American Bar Association

Max Zimny, Co-Chair
General Counsel, International Ladies' Garment Workers' Union
Representative, Council of Labor and Employment Section, American Bar Association

Arnold Zack, Co-Chair
President, National Academy of Arbitrators

Carl E. VerBeek
Management Co-Chair, Union Co-Chair
Partner, Varnum, Riddering, Schmidt & Howlett
Arbitration Committee of Labor and Employment Section, American
Bar Association

Robert D. Manning
Angoff, Goldman, Manning, Pyle, Wanger & Hiatt, P.C.
Union Co-Chair
Arbitration Committee of Labor and Employment Section, American
Bar Association

Charles F. Ipavec, Arbitrator
Neutral Co-Chair
Arbitration Committee of Labor and Employment Section, American
Bar Association

George H. Friedman
Senior Vice President, American Arbitration Association

Michael F. Hoellering
General Counsel, American Arbitration Association

W. Bruce Newman
Representative, Society of Professionals in Dispute Resolution

Wilma Liebman
Special Assistant to the Director, Federal Mediation and Conciliation
Service

Joseph Garrison
President, National Employment Lawyers Association

Lewis Maltby
Director, Workplace Rights Project, American Civil Liberties Union

Appendix C

Massachusetts Commission Against Discrimination Policy 96–1

Policy on Alternative Dispute Resolution

Michael T. Duffy, Chairman
Dorca I. Gomez, Commissioner
Charles E. Walker Jr., Commissioner
February 14, 1996

The Massachusetts Commission Against Discrimination (MCAD) is committed to providing arbitration, mediation and other forms of Alternative Dispute Resolution (ADR) to Complainants and Respondents who choose them. With a growing number of new complaints filed each year, arbitration and mediation provide low-cost and expedited avenues of bringing discrimination cases to an equitable conclusion. ADR is tenable only where minimum standards of quality and procedural safeguards insure just and fair processes and outcomes; this *Policy on Alternative Dispute Resolution* represents the Commission's commitment to establish such standards.

The MCAD is one of the first civil rights enforcement agencies in the country to comprehensively employ ADR to resolve cases. It is likely that the policy outlined herein will evolve and change as the Commission gains more experience and insight into the uses and limits of Alternative Dispute Resolution. A formal evaluation of the experience with this policy will be conducted drawing on information to be collected from each case submitted to ADR. Comparisons will be made to cases that are resolved through standard Commission procedures. Among the criteria to be used in evaluating this policy will be the effects on the time required to

179

resolve a case, the costs to the parties and the Commission, and the satisfaction of the parties with the process.

This document represents a first step in describing the Commission's policy with regard to ADR and may be modified by additional policy bulletins; it will likely be codified through regulation after a trial period and eventually, perhaps, translated into statute.

I. Arbitration

Arbitration is the process by which parties to a dispute select a third party neutral to render a binding decision as to the outcome of a dispute. By adopting a policy which allows for the arbitration of discrimination claims, the Commission will be vesting third party neutrals with considerable powers. Because of this, and because of the important social values embodied in discrimination law, strict parameters will be placed on the circumstances under which Commission sanctioned arbitration will take place. Those parameters are described below.

1. *Choosing Arbitration*

(a) Cases will only be submitted to binding arbitration where both Complainant and Respondent voluntarily agree to do so, and where both parties have had the opportunity to confer with counsel. Further, both Complainant and Respondent must agree on who will arbitrate their dispute or agree on the means by which an arbitrator will be selected.

(b) When the parties choose arbitration, the processing of a complaint by the MCAD will be suspended; the case will be closed by the Commission once the arbitrator renders a decision.

(c) The processing of a complaint will be suspended at the time the parties file a written agreement to arbitrate with the Clerk of the Commission incorporating all of the arbitration protocols outlined in this policy bulletin. In order for the agreement to be effective, it must be signed by the Commissioner assigned to the case.

The MCAD will not recognize those arbitrations that do not incorporate the protocols outlined in this policy bulletin.

(d) The MCAD will not recognize those arbitration agreements that come as a result of mandatory arbitration provisions that employees are required to sign as a condition of employment, or are imposed prior to a dispute arising.

(e) Arbitration is probably most appropriate after the Commission has investigated a complaint of discrimination and found probable cause. However, the Commission will recognize any arbitration regardless of what stage of the process a complaint is in, when both parties agree to it, both parties are represented by counsel, and the arbitration proceeds according to the protocols outlined in this bulletin.

2. *Representation by Counsel*

(a) The Commission will not recognize claims that are arbitrated where either Complainant or Respondent does not have the advice of counsel.

(b) Where the Commission has found Probable Cause, and where a Complainant is *pro se*, the Commission will assign an MCAD staff attorney to present the Complainant's case before an arbitrator. Complainants always have the right to decline the services of Commission counsel and retain representation of their own choosing. For the limited purposes of the reference in G.L. c. 151B, sec. 5 pertaining to the role of Commission attorneys where a Complainant is pro se, the arbitration proceeding shall be deemed to be a Commission proceeding.

3. *Roster of Arbitrators*

(a) The MCAD will recognize only those decisions rendered by arbitrators deemed to be knowledgeable and experienced by the Commission. A roster will be maintained of all such arbitrators recognized by the MCAD.

(b) The parties will be presented with the roster of arbitrators recognized by the MCAD, listing the arbitrator's name, area of practice, background, evaluations from other parties who have used the arbitrator's services and category of cases they are deemed qualified to arbitrate (see 4(c) below). The choice of an arbitrator, or how an arbitrator will be chosen, will be up to the parties. If the parties cannot agree on an arbitrator, they may request that the MCAD (or a subcontractor designated by the MCAD) appoint an arbitrator from the roster.

(c) Administration of the roster may be contracted by the MCAD to a qualified subcontractor, though the Commission reserves all rights to set standards and otherwise implement these policy guidelines.

(d) Arbitrators shall conform their conduct in any arbitration referred to them by the MCAD to the Code of Ethics for Arbitrators promulgated by the American Arbitration Association and the American Bar Association. The MCAD, or a third party contractor, shall make copies of these standards available upon request.

4. *Qualifications of Arbitrators*

(a) In determining whether to list an individual on the MCAD's arbitration roster, the Commission will examine a variety of factors, though no one factor may be necessarily determinative. Generally, the Commission would examine the ability of the individual to fairly and efficiently administer, manage and control an evidentiary proceeding which though adjudicatory in nature, is less formal than a public hearing. The Commission will also examine the familiarity of the applicant with contemporary standards employed by the courts with regard to discrimination law.

(b) The following are examples of the factors that will be reviewed by the Commission in determining whether an applicant should be listed on the MCAD roster of arbitrators:

i. The applicant's civil litigation experience, as demonstrated by the following:

  a. Superior Court or US District Court trial work, of any nature, involving jury trials and/or bench trials.

  b. Judicial (any level) or Administrative (any forum) trial work, focusing on issues arising under the MCAD's or EEOC's jurisdiction, involving matters focusing on discrimination in housing, employment or public accommodations; and a record of serving as counsel in at least one appellate matter (any court) involving issues of housing, employment, or public accommodations.

  c. Appellate matters involving issues arising under G.L. c. 151B, together with a record demonstrating that the applicant has trial experience in any forum satisfactory to the Commission.

  d. A record of civil or criminal litigation experience involving matters in any forum.

ii. Experience as an arbitrator or hearing officer in other matters.

iii. Evidence of a professional career which demonstrates that the applicant has the temperament and personal background sufficient to perform the duties of an arbitrator.

iv. Good references.

v. Completion of an MCAD annual training and evaluation program.

vi. Other experience that, in the opinion of the Commissioners demonstrates evidence of familiarity with civil rights statutes and their enforcement.

(c) Arbitrators may be deemed, depending on their particular experience, qualified by the MCAD for one or more of the following categories of cases: housing;

public accommodations; employment—disability; employment—sex; employment—national origin/ancestry; employment—race; employment—religion; employment—sexual orientation; employment—retaliation.

(d) If upon review, prospective arbitrators are determined to lack the requisite experience to be listed on an MCAD roster, they may substitute a course of training and study to re-apply and become listed. The course of training and study must be approved by the Commission, and successfully completed by the applicant.

(e) The Commission will take affirmative steps to insure that the roster of arbitrators contains professionals with a broad diversity of backgrounds.

(f) Arbitrators have a duty to disclose to the parties any relationship which might reasonably constitute or be perceived as a conflict of interest.

5. *Fees for Arbitration*

(a) The fees charged for arbitration shall be allocated amongst the parties in a manner which they deem to be fair and equitable. In some instances, this may require one party to pay a higher percentage than that paid by the other party, or shall require one party to pay the full fee; where possible, both parties should make some contribution toward the fee.

(b) Where the Commission has delegated administration of the roster to a third party contractor, the contractor may take a role in allocating the payment of the fee between the parties.

(c) The arbitrator shall not be informed of how the fee was allocated, and shall be paid either through the Commission or through a third party contractor.

6. *Discovery*

(a) Parties who elect arbitration will have a limited opportunity for discovery prior to submitting the case to an arbitrator. The period for discovery will run thirty days from the day the parties formally elect arbitration. The scope of discovery is at the discretion of the arbitrator.

(b) The arbitrator may cause subpoenas to be issued for the attendance of witnesses and for the production of books, records, documents and other evidence, and shall have the power to administer oaths. On application of a party and a showing of good cause, the arbitrator may permit depositions to be taken.

(c) Each side must produce to the other any documents which it intends to introduce at arbitration. With approval from the arbitrator, any party in an arbitration proceeding may serve upon any other party a request for the production of documents as permitted by rule thirty-four of the Massachusetts Rules of Civil Procedure.

7. *The Arbitration Proceeding and Decision*

(a) The parties must produce a record (stenographic or cassette tape) of the arbitration proceeding at their own expense. Witnesses who testify must do so under oath. Information will be allowed into evidence only at the discretion of the arbitrator. The arbitrator shall be the judge of relevance and materiality of the evidence offered and conformity to the rules of evidence shall not be required. All evidence shall be taken in the presence of both parties.

(b) The arbitrator shall appoint a time and place for the hearing and cause written notice to the parties to be served personally or by registered mail not less than ten days before the hearing. The parties shall have the right to be heard, to present evidence material to the controversy and to cross-examine witnesses appearing at the hearing. The arbitrator shall hear and determine the controversy upon the evidence produced.

(c) The arbitrator may impose any remedies that would be available under Massachusetts General Laws Chapter 151B, unless the parties agree in advance of the arbitration, in writing, to constraints on the arbitrator's discretion. One example of the constraints the parties might agree to, would be the imposition of upper and/or lower limits on the size of a damage award.

(d) The arbitrator shall issue a written decision explaining the rationale for the result they reached within thirty days of the close of the arbitration proceeding. The decision, along with a copy of the record, shall be filed with the Clerk of the Commission.

8. *Review by the Commission*

(a) Thirty business days after the decision of the arbitrator is filed at the Commission, the decision will become final and binding on the parties and the case will be closed. Before thirty days have elapsed, the decision may be set aside by an order of two Commissioners of the MCAD. The Commissioners may set the decision aside if, after reviewing it, they believe the decision is not in the public interest based on the following criteria:

i.   the award was procured by corruption, fraud or other undue means;

ii.   there was evident partiality by an arbitrator appointed as a neutral, corruption of the arbitrator or misconduct prejudicing the rights of any party;

iii. the arbitrator exceeded their powers or refused to hear evidence material to the issues in dispute;

iv.   the decision of the arbitrator is palpably wrong and/or is clearly repugnant to the purposes and policies of the Commission;

v.   every reasonable presumption will be made in favor of the award.

If a decision is set aside by the Commissioners, the complaint shall be reinstated at the Commission back to the point at which the parties elected arbitration and will then proceed along the normal course to adjudication. The arbitrator's decision, as well as the record of the arbitration proceeding, will be admissible at a public hearing if the case is reinstated at the Commission.

(b) Upon application made within thirty days after delivery of a copy of the award to the applicant, the Commission shall modify or correct the award if:

 i. there was an evident miscalculation of figures or an evident mistake in the description of any person, thing or property referred to in the award;

 ii. the award is imperfect in a matter of form, not affecting the merits of the controversy.

If the application is granted, the Commission shall modify and correct the award so as to effect its intent and shall confirm the award as so modified and corrected.

9. *Non-Binding Arbitration*

(a) Parties may agree to submit their dispute to non-binding arbitration by mutual agreement before the commencement of an arbitration proceeding. All of the parameters outlined with regard to binding arbitration in sections 1–8, apply to non-binding arbitration, except that the party dissatisfied with the arbitrator's decision must pay the legal fees and costs incurred by the opposing side in the course of litigating the case in arbitration, in full, before the case will be reinstated. If a party elects to reinstate the case at the Commission they must do so within thirty days of the issuance of the decision.

(b) The arbitrator's decision, as well as the record of the arbitration proceeding, will be admissible at a public hearing if the case is reinstated at the Commission.

II. *Mediation*

Mediation is the process by which the parties to a dispute voluntarily attempt to resolve their differences with the assistance of a third party neutral. Ultimately resolving a complaint through mediation is entirely dependent on both parties entering into a mutually agreeable settlement. Unlike arbitration, the third party neutral has no power to unilaterally impose a decision on the parties, and therefore the strict parameters that govern arbitration need not apply to mediation. Nevertheless, some parameters should attend the mediation of complaints of discrimination at the MCAD; they are set forth below.

1. *Choosing Mediation*
   (a) Cases will only be mediated where both Complainant and Respondent voluntarily agree to do so. Further, the parties must agree on who will mediate their dispute or agree on the means by which a mediator will be selected.

2. *Roster of Mediators*
   (a) The Commission will maintain a roster of mediators determined to be knowledgeable and experienced; in listing mediators on the roster the MCAD will use the same factors that are used for arbitrators, described in Section I(4). The parties are not required to use mediators who are listed on an MCAD roster but may find it useful to do so.
   (b) An additional factor for inclusion on the roster of mediators is the successful completion of mediation training that will have the effect of invoking the statutory protections of the Mediation Confidentiality Statute, M.G.L. c. 233, s. 23C. As with arbitrators, mediators will be required to complete an annual training and evaluation program.
   (c) Depending on their particular experience, mediators may be deemed qualified by the MCAD for one or more of the following categories of cases: housing; public accommodations; employment—disability; employment—sex; employment—national origin/ancestry; employment—race; employment—religion; employment—sexual orientation; employment—retaliation.

(d) If upon review, prospective mediators are determined to lack the requisite experience to be listed on an MCAD roster, they may substitute a course of training and study to re-apply to become listed. The course of training and study must be approved by the Commission, and must be successfully completed by the applicant.

(e) The Commission will take affirmative steps to insure that the roster of mediators contains professionals with a broad diversity of backgrounds.

(f) Mediators have a duty to disclose to the parties any relationship which might reasonably constitute or be perceived as a conflict of interest.

(g) Mediators shall conform their conduct in any mediation referred to them by the MCAD to the Model Standards of Conduct for Mediators promulgated by the American Arbitration Association, American Bar Association, and Society of Professionals in Dispute Resolution. The MCAD, or a third party contractor, shall make copies of these standards available upon request.

3. *Fees for Mediators*

(a) The fees charged for mediation shall be allocated amongst the parties in a manner which they deem to be fair and equitable. In some instances, this may require one party to pay a higher percentage than that paid by the other party, or shall require one party to pay the full fee; where possible, both parties should make some contribution toward the fee.

(b) Where the Commission has delegated administration of the roster to a third party contractor, the contractor may take a role in allocating the payment of the fee between the parties.

(c) The mediator shall not be informed of how the fee was allocated, and shall be paid through the Commission or through a third party contractor.

4. *Review by the Commission*

   (a) Settlement agreements arrived at through mediation must be submitted to the MCAD for approval before a case will be closed by the Commission. The decision to approve a settlement agreement and close the case may be made by the Investigating Commissioner assigned to the case, if the complaint is still under investigation and no finding of probable cause has been made; or may be made by the Hearing Commissioner if a finding of probable cause has been made and the case has been certified for public hearing.

   (b) The grounds upon which the assigned Commissioner may decline to recognize a settlement agreement and keep the case open at the Commission include:

       i.   One of the parties was represented by counsel.

       ii. The terms of the settlement agreement are at a substantial variance with the outcomes of other cases with similar fact patterns and a reasonable explanation is lacking.

       iii. The public interest requires the Commission to keep the case open.

   (c) The MCAD may close a case for failure to cooperate where the assigned Commissioner believes the Complainant is refusing to accept a good faith offer from the Respondent that would make the Complainant whole.

   (d) The mediation proceeding, the positions of the parties expressed during the mediation, offers and counteroffers made during the mediation, shall be confidential and shall be inadmissible in any subsequent proceedings at the Commission or in Court.

Arbitration and mediation may be attractive alternatives for many of the Complainants and Respondents who have claims pending at the Massachusetts Commission Against Discrimination. It will not however, provide a complete substitute for the process of formal adjudication for every case. The MCAD will continue to resolve any and all cases where the parties do not choose arbitration or mediation, at the same time it provides alternatives to those who do want them.

In addition to the ADR alternatives provided by the MCAD once a complaint has been filed, the Commission strongly supports the expansion and development of in-house alternative workplace dispute resolution mechanisms. Such systems should be voluntary and should operate within the standards of fairness detailed in the guidelines above. Doing so will help to eliminate the conditions that give rise to claims of discrimination and will resolve those that do arise, in a just and efficient manner.

In drafting this policy, the Commission acknowledges its gratitude to the following organizations and individuals for the information and guidance they have provided; their inclusion on this list should not necessarily be construed as their endorsement of this policy, only as a sign of the Commission's gratitude for their assistance: the *Task Force on Alternative Dispute Resolution in Employment* and their *Due Process Protocol for Mediation and Arbitration of Statutory Disputes Arising Out of the Employment Relationship* issued on May 9, 1995; the *Report and Recommendations* issued by the *Commission on the Future of Worker-Management Relations* under the auspices of the US Departments of Labor and Commerce in December of 1994; *Dr. John T. Dunlop*, Former Secretary of Labor, and Lamont University Professor Emeritus at Harvard University; *Arnold Zack*, former President of the National Academy of Arbitrators; *Fredie Kay*, Executive Director of the Massachusetts Office of Dispute Resolution; *Attorneys Dalia Rudavsky* and *Wendy Kaplan*, of the National Employment Lawyers Association (NELA); *Attorney Rick Ward*, of the law firm of Ropes & Gray; *Attorney Arthur Telegen*, of the law firm of Foley, Hoag & Eliot; *Dr. Lamont Stallworth*, Founder and Chairman of the Center for Employment Dispute Resolution; *Attorney David Hoffman*, of the law firm of Hill & Barlow; *Jay Siegel*, faculty member at the John F. Kennedy School of Government at Harvard University; *John Wallace*, President of

ADR/Equimar; *Douglas McDowell*, General Counsel for the Equal Employment Advisory Council; *Ericka Gray*, of JAMS/Endispute; and finally, *Thomas A. Kochan*, George M. Bunker Professor of Management at the Massachusetts Institute of Technology.

Notes

Chapter One

1. *Spielberg Mfg. Co.*, 112 NLRB 1080 (1955).
2. Cox, A., *Law and the National Labor Policy*, Los Angeles: Institute of Industrial Relations, University of California, 1960, p. 64.
3. Fleming, R., *The Arbitration Process*, Urbana, Ill.: University of Illinois Press, 1965, pp. 23–27; *United Steelworkers of America v. Warrior and Gulf Navigation Co.*, 363 US 574.
4. Kellor, F., *Arbitration in the New Industrial Society*, New York: McGraw-Hill, 1934, pp. 20–31.
5. Witte, E., *Historical Survey of Labor Arbitration*, Philadelphia: University of Pennsylvania Press, 1952, p. 4.
6. Webb, S., and Webb, B., *Industrial Democracy*, London: Longmans, Green, 1914, p. 223, note 2. See also Coleman, S. and Haynes, T., *Labor Arbitration: An Annotated Bibliography*, Ithaca, N.Y.: ILR Press, 1994.
7. Commons, J., and Associates, *History of Labor in the United States*, Vol. II, New York: Macmillan, 1936, p. 326.
8. Mitchell, J., *Organized Labor: The Problems, Purposes and Ideals and the Present and Future of American Wage Earners*, Philadelphia: American Book and Bible House, 1903, p. 351.
9. For further discussion, see Cox, A., and Dunlop, J., "Regulation of Collective Bargaining by the National Labor Relations Board" and "The Duty to Bargain Collectively During the Term of an Existing Agreement," *Harvard Law Review*, 63(3), 1950, 389–432 and 63(7), 1950, 1097–1133.

10. Dunlop, J., and Chamberlain, N., eds., *Frontiers of Collective Bargaining*, New York: HarperCollins, 1967, pp. 103–121.

11. Witte, *Historical Survey*, pp. 22–23.

12. Blackman, J., *Presidential Seizure in Labor Disputes*, Cambridge, Mass.: Harvard University Press, 1967, pp. 257–281.

13. 39 sTATA.721. Constitutionality of the Act was sustained by the Supreme Court in 1917 (*Wilson v. New*, 243 US 332).

14. Congressional intervention has been used in thirteen instances of disputes on the railroads in the period 1963–1996. There have been a total of seventy-four emergency boards in the railroad industry in the same period, twenty-three of which have been in commuter railroads under Section 9(a).

15. Witte, E., *The Government in Labor Disputes*, New York: McGraw-Hill, 1932, p. 253.

16. Mulliken, O., *The Massachusetts Board of Conciliation and Arbitration*, unpublished Ph.D. dissertation, Division of History, Government, and Economics, Harvard University, 1942. (Harvard University Archives). Mulliken notes that between 1918 and 1935 the Board handled 594 conciliation cases and 3390 arbitration cases (p. 12). Also see Brown, L., S. J., *Union Policies in the Leather Industry*, Cambridge, Mass.: Harvard University Press, 1947, pp. 192–201. In the period 1933–1940 the Board handled 358 arbitration cases and 139 conciliation cases in the leather industry.

17. See Braun, K., *The Settlement of Industrial Disputes*, Philadelphia: Blakiston, 1944, pp. 145–148.

18. *Encyclopedia of the Social Sciences*, New York, 1930, Vol. V, p. 165. Millis, H., and Montgomery, R., however, regarded conciliation as the adjustment of disputes by the parties in interest, and mediation to be the intervention of an outside person. *Organized Labor*, New York: McGraw-Hill, 1945, p. 719, note 2. For a definitive discussion of mediation, see Simkin, W., *Mediation and the Dynamics of Collective Bargaining*, Washington, D.C.: Bureau of National Affairs, 1971; 2nd ed., 1986,

with Fidandis, N. For an analytic discussion of mediation, see Dunlop, J., *Dispute Resolution, Negotiation and Consensus Building*, Westport, Conn.: Auburn House, 1984, pp. 22–25.

19. *The Ohio Public Employee Collective Bargaining Act and Administrative Rules of the State Employment Relations Board*, 1995, pp. 59–61.

20. See Suffern, A., *Conciliation and Arbitration in the Coal Industry of America*, Boston: Houghton Mifflin, 1915, pp. 256–57; Fisher, W., "Anthracite," in *How Collective Bargaining Works*, New York: Twentieth Century Fund, 1942, pp. 280–317.

21. Fleming, *The Arbitration Process*, p. 6.

22. Robinson, D., *Collective Bargaining and Market Control in the New York Coat and Suit Industry*, New York: Columbia University Press, 1949, pp. 65–101.

23. Kennedy, T., *Effective Labor Arbitration: The Impartial Chairmanship of the Full-Fashioned Hosiery Industry*, Philadelphia: University of Pennsylvania Press, 1948.

24. Wolf, H., "Railroads," in *How Collective Bargaining Works*, 1942, p. 327.

25. See Commission on the Future of Worker-Management Relations, *Fact Finding Report*, Washington, D.C.: U.S. Department of Labor, May 1994, p. 99.

26. Burns, R., "Daily Newspapers," in *How Collective Bargaining Works*, 1942, pp. 52–64.

27. Millis, H., and Montgomery, R., *Organized Labor*, New York: McGraw-Hill, 1945, p. 101. Also refer to Perlman, S., and Taft, P., *History of Labor in the United States, 1896–1932*, Vol. IV, New York: Macmillan, 1935, pp. 48–49.

28. Lowell, J., *Industrial Arbitration and Conciliation*, New York: Putnam, 1893, pp. 81–89.

29. Montgomery, R., *Industrial Relations in the Chicago Building Trades*, Chicago: University of Chicago Press, 1927, pp. 84–87.

30. Montgomery, *Industrial Relations*, pp. 233–69.

31. Troy, L., *Trade Union Membership, 1897–1962*, Occasional

Paper 92, National Bureau of Economic Research, New York: Columbia University Press, 1965, p. 1. These data exclude Canadian membership.

32. *The Termination Report, National War Labor Board*, Vol. 1, Washington, D.C.: U.S. Department of Labor, 1947, p. 66. Also see Taylor, G., *Government Regulation and Industrial Relations*, Englewood Cliffs, N.J.: Prentice Hall, 1948.

33. "Grievance Procedures," in *Termination Report*, pp. 104–134. This chapter details the range of issues and cases in which the Board implemented its general policy.

34. "Labor Organizations and Conferences," *Monthly Labor Review*, 1946, 62(1), 37–43.

35. Slichter, S., Healy, J., and Livernash, R., *The Impact of Collective Bargaining on Management*, Washington, D.C.: Brookings Institution, 1960, p. 739.

36. See Witte, *The Government in Labor Disputes*, p. 45.

37. See Cole, D. L., *The Quest for Industrial Peace*, Meyer Kestnbaum Lectures, New York: McGraw-Hill, 1963, pp. 69–94.

38. Shils, E., Gershenfeld, W., Ingater, B., and Weinberg, W., *Industrial Peacemaker: George W. Taylor's Contributions to Collective Bargaining*, Philadelphia: University of Pennsylvania, 1979;"George W. Taylor: Industrial Peacemaker," *Monthly Labor Review*, Dec. 1995, pp. 29–34. Following a period as umpire in the hosiery industry, he served as second umpire under the UAW-General Motors agreement before becoming vice-chairman of the War Labor Board.

39. Leiserson, W., *Right and Wrong in Labor Relations*, Berkeley: University of California Press, 1942. Leiserson served as umpire in the clothing industry in Rochester, New York. He was chairman of the National Mediation Board and also served as chairman of the National Labor Relations Board.

40. Harry A. Millis served as arbitrator in the Chicago men's clothing industry and as the first umpire under the General Motors-

UAW agreement. He was also chairman of the National Labor Relations Board.

41. For an account of some of these careers, see Friedman, C., *Between Labor and Management: Oral Histories of Arbitration*, New York: Twayne, 1995; Yaffe, B., ed., *The Saul Wallen Papers: A Neutral's Contribution to Industrial Peace*, Ithaca: New York State School of Industrial and Labor Relations, 1974. For a discussion of substantive and procedural issues confronting arbitrators, see the annual proceedings of the National Academy of Arbitrators; also see Bognanno, M., and Coleman, C., *Labor Arbitration in America: The Profession in Practice*, New York: Praeger, 1992.

42. *Textile Workers v. Lincoln Mills*, 353 US 448, 455 (1957).

43. *Daily Labor Report*, Washington, D.C.: Bureau of National Affairs, Feb. 12, 1996, p. D–4. The data are from a Bureau of Labor Statistics release of Feb. 9, 1996.

44. In 1976, the Bureau of Labor Statistics reported that nine out of ten state and local government agreements contained some form of contractual grievance procedure, and of these, 85 percent culminated in arbitration. Bureau of Labor Statistics, "Collective Bargaining Agreements for State and County Government Employees," bulletin no. 1920, Washington, D.C., 1976. Also see bulletin no. 1833, "Grievance and Arbitration Procedures in State and Local Government," 1985. The Bureau of Labor Statistics has made no more recent study on this subject.

45. For an account of labor-management relations in state and local government, see *Working Together for Public Service*, Report of the U.S. Secretary of Labor's Task Force on Excellence in State and Local Government Through Labor-Management Cooperation, U.S. Department of Labor, Washington, D.C.: Government Printing Office, 1996. For the federal government, see Vice President Al Gore, *From Red Tape to Results: Creating a Government that Works Better and Costs Less*, Report

of the National Performance Review, Washington, D.C.: Government Printing Office, 1993.

46. Ziskind, D., *One Thousand Strikes of Government Employees*, New York: Columbia University Press, 1940, pp. 55–58.

47. Ziskind, *One Thousand Strikes*, p. 22.

48. Cited in Spero, S., *Government as Employer*, New York: Remsen Press, 1948, p. 407.

49. Spero, *Government as Employer*, p. 2.

50. Schneider, B., "Public-Sector Labor Legislation—An Evolutionary Analysis," in *Public Sector Bargaining*, 2nd ed., edited by B. Aaron, J. M. Najita, and J. L. Stern, Industrial Relations Research Association, Washington, D.C.: Bureau of National Affairs, 1988, p. 195.

51. Brock, J. *Bargaining Beyond Impasse: Joint Resolution of Public Sector Disputes*, Westport, Conn.: Auburn House, 1982.

52. Governor's Committee on Public Employee Relations, *Final Report*, State of New York, March 31, 1966. J. Dunlop was a member of the Taylor Committee appointed by Governor Rockefeller.

53. New York State, Public Employment Relations Board, Vol. 29, no. 4, *1995–96 Annual Report Edition*, p. 3.

54. Walsh, J., and Mangum, G., *Labor Struggle in the Post Office: From Selective Lobbying to Collective Bargaining*, Armonk, N.Y.: Sharpe, 1992, pp. 97–232; Stern, J., "Unionism in the Public Sector," in *Public Sector Bargaining*, pp. 53–64.

55. Freeman, R., and Ichniowski, C., eds., *When Public Sector Workers Organize*, Chicago: University of Chicago Press, 1988.

56. *Public Employees Bargain for Excellence: A Compendium of State Public Sector Labor Relations Laws*, Public Employee Department, AFL-CIO, Washington, D.C., 1995.

57. Walsh and Mangum, *Labor Struggle in the Post Office*, p. 198.

58. For a comparison with arbitration in Britain, see Mumford, K., "Arbitration and ACAS in Britain: A Historical Perspective," *British Journal of Industrial Relations*, 1996, 34(2), 287–305.

59. Compare, for example, the operations of the Chrysler, Ford,

and General Motors dispute-settling arrangements under similar agreements with the UAW. See Alexander, G., "Impartial Umpires, The General Motors-UAW Case," *Proceedings of the Twelfth Annual Meeting, National Academy of Arbitrators*, Washington, D.C.: Bureau of National Affairs, 1959, pp. 108–60; Wolff, D., Crane, L., and Cole, H., "The Chrysler-UAW Umpire System," *Proceedings of the Eleventh Annual Meeting, National Academy of Arbitrators*, Washington, D.C.: Bureau of National Affairs, 1958, pp. 111–148; also see Harry Shulman, "Reason, Contract, and Law in Labor Relations," *Proceedings of the Ninth Annual Meeting, National Academy of Arbitrators*, Washington, D.C.: Bureau of National Affairs, 1956. Shulman was impartial umpire under the Ford-UAW agreement.

Chapter Two

1. Cooper, L., and Nolan, D., *Labor Arbitration: A Coursebook*, St. Paul, Minn.: West, 1994, pp. 258–284.
2. See Elkouri F., and Elkouri, E. A., *How Arbitration Works*, 4th ed., Washington, D.C.: Bureau of National Affairs, 1985. Chapter 4 describes the various forms of arbitration tribunals.
3. Bognano, M., and Coleman, C., *Labor Arbitration in America: The Profession and Practice*, New York: Praeger, 1992.
4. *Spielberg Mfg. Co.*, 112 NLRB 1080 (1955), provides an interesting illustration of this policy in action.
5. Elkouri and Elkouri, *How Arbitration Works*, pp. 19–20.
6. Mittenthal, R., "Self-Interest: Arbitration's Unmentionable Consideration," *Dispute Resolution Journal*, Mar. 1994, pp. 70–72.
7. *Alexander v. Gardner-Denver*, 415 US 36 (1974).
8. *Gilmer v. Interstate/Johnson Lane Corp.*, 500 US 20 (1991).

Chapter Three

1. Landis, J., *The Administrative Process*, New Haven, Conn.: Yale University Press, 1938, p. 1; McCraw, T., *Prophets of Regulation*,

Cambridge, Mass.: Belnap Press of Harvard University Press, 1984, pp. 153, 201.

2. Landis, J. *The Administrative Process*, p. 46. The other two quotations in this paragraph are from *Ibid.*, p. 4.

3. 86 Cong Rec 13, 942–43 (1940). Quoted in Harter, P., "Dispute Resolution and Administrative Law: The History, Needs, and Future of a Complex Relationship," *Villanova Law Review*, 1983–84, 29, 1400–1401.

4. Landis, J., *Report on Regulatory Agencies to the President-Elect*, U.S. Senate, Committee on the Judiciary, 86th Cong. 2nd Sess., Washington, D.C.: Government Printing Office, 1960.

5. McCraw, *Prophets of Regulation*, p. 220.

6. Meyer, J., Peck, M., Stenson, J., and Zwick, C., *The Economics of Competition in the Transportation Industries*, Cambridge, Mass.: Harvard University Press, 1959; MacAvoy, P., ed., *The Crisis of the Regulatory Commissions*, New York: Norton, 1970. Also see Breyer, S. *Regulation and Its Reform*, Cambridge, Mass.: Harvard University Press, 1982.

7. See, however, Reynolds, M., "A New Paradigm: Deregulating Labor Relations," *Journal of Labor Research*, 1996, XVII(1), 121–127. "Recent successes with deregulation in product markets suggest that we can deregulate labor relations and replace the vast labor codes (over 400,000 NLRB pages alone) with labor market competition and common law." Also see Yager, D. V., *NLRB Agency in Crisis*, Washington, D.C.: Labor Policy Association, 1996.

8. Administrative Conference of the United States, *Toward Improved Agency Dispute Resolution: Implementing the ADR Act*, Report of the Administrative Conference of the United States on Agency Implementation of the Administrative Dispute Resolution Act, Thomasina V. Rogers, Chair, Washington, D.C., Feb. 1995. See especially p. 4, "What is ADR?"

9. Commission on the Future of Worker-Management Relations, *Report and Recommendations*, Dec. 1994, Washington, D.C.:

U.S. Department of Labor, p. 45.

10. For the reactions of managers and workers to this legislated complex applicable to the workplace, see U.S. General Accounting Office, *Workplace Regulation Information on Selected Employer and Union Experiences*, vols. I and II, Washington, D.C., June 1994.

11. Commission on the Future of Worker-Management Relations, *Fact Finding Report*, May 1994, p. 134.

12. Commission on the Future of Worker-Management Relations, *Report and Recommendations*, Dec. 1994, p. 54.

13. Bureau of National Affairs, *Daily Labor Report*, January 17, 1997, p. S-19.

14. Administrative Conference of the United States, *Toward Improved Agency Dispute Resolution*, Feb. 1995.

15. See Commission on the Future of Worker-Management Relations, *Fact Finding Report*, May, 1994, pp. 116–117.

16. Commission on the Future of Worker-Management Relations, *Report and Recommendations*, Dec. 1994, pp. 30–33.

17. *Spielberg Mfg. Co.*, 112 NLRB 1080 (1955), and *Raytheon Corp.*, 140 NLRB 883 (1963). See Siegel, J., "Changing Public Policy: Private Arbitration to Resolve Statutory Employment Disputes," to be published in *The Labor Lawyer*, *13*(1), Summer 1997.

18. *United Technologies Corp.*, 268 NLRB 557 (1984).

19. PL 101–552, as amended by PL 102–354, sunset by the provision of Section 11 in October 1995. The Administrative Dispute Resolution Act of 1996 provides in Section 9 a permanent authorization of alternative dispute resolution.

20. *Report to the Secretary of Labor on the Philadelphia ADR Pilot Project* (Oct. 1992); Schuyler, M., *A Cost Analysis of the Department of Labor's Philadelphia ADR Pilot Project*, Washington, D.C.: U.S. Department of Labor (Aug. 1993).

21. McEwen, C., and Bowdoin College, "An Evaluation of the Equal Employment Opportunity Commission's Pilot Mediation

Program," March 1994, Washington, D.C.: EEOC, unpublished.

22. See Equal Employment Opportunity Commission, Task Force on Alternative Dispute Resolution, *Report to Gilbert F. Casellas*, Submitted by Commissioners R. Gaull Silberman and Paul Steven Miller, March 1995; Equal Employment Opportunity Commission, "Alternative Dispute Resolution Policy Statement," July 17, 1995.

23. See Interagency Agreement between Federal Mediation and Conciliation Service and the Equal Employment Opportunity Commission, 1996; "Many Attorneys Welcome EEOC Decisions to Refer Charges to Federal Mediators," *Daily Labor Report*, Washington, D.C.: Bureau of National Affairs, Oct. 16, 1996, pp. A8–9.

24. U.S. General Accounting Office, *Employment Discrimination: Most Private-Sector Employers Use Alternative Dispute Resolution*, Washington, D.C., July 1995.

25. *Working Together for Public Service*, pp. 80–83; 181–186.

26. Massachusetts Commission Against Discrimination, *Policy on Alternative Dispute Resolution*, Policy 96–1, Feb. 14, 1996.

27. See ACUS Recommendation 82–4 and 85–5, Administrative Conference of the United States, *Negotiated Rulemaking Sourcebook*, Washington, D.C., 1990, pp. 1, 11–19.

28. Dunlop, J., "The Limits of Legal Compulsion," *Labor Law Journal*, 1976, *27*(2), 67. This article was originally developed as a memorandum distributed to Department of Labor staff and other agencies in 1975.

29. Dunlop, "The Limits of Legal Compulsion," p. 74.

30. For a more detailed account, see Perritt, H., "Negotiated Rulemaking Before Federal Agencies: Evaluation of Recommendations by the Administrative Conference of the United States," *Georgetown Law Journal Association*, 1986, *74*, particularly pp. 1630–1636; also Perritt, H., "Administrative Alternative Dispute Resolution: The Development of Negotiated Rulemaking and Other Processes," *Pepperdine Law Review*, 1987, *14*, partic-

ularly pp. 611–615. These articles are reprinted in major part in Administrative Conference of the United States, *Negotiated Rulemaking Sourcebook*, pp. 554–602; 603–660.

31. Stewart, R., "The Reformation of American Administrative Law," *Harvard Law Review*, 1975, 88, 1667–1813.

32. Stewart, "The Reformation of American Administrative Law," p. 1670.

33. Sander, F., "The Variety of Dispute Resolution," 70 Federal Rules Decisions 111 (1976).

34. Harter, P., "Negotiating Regulations: A Cure for Malaise," *Georgetown Law Journal Association*, 1982, 71, 1–113. Also see Harter, P., "Points on a Continuum: Dispute Resolution Procedures and the Administrative Process," *American University Administrative Law Journal*, 1987, 1, 141–211.

35. ICFR 305.82-2. Also see "Experienced Practitioner Offers Guidance to Participants in Negotiated Rulemaking," reprinted in Administrative Conference in the United States, *Negotiated Rulemaking Sourcebook*, 1990, pp. 544–553.

36. January 24, 1983, 68 *American Bar Association Journal* 274, 275 (1982).

37. Perritt, "Administrative Alternative Dispute Resolution," p. 874.

38. *NEA Notes*, 1996, 27(6), 1.

39. Statement of Joseph A. Dear Before the House Judiciary Subcommittee on Commercial and Administrative Law, June 27, 1996.

40. Commission on the Future of Worker-Management Relations, *Fact-Finding Report*, May 1994, Washington, D.C.: U.S. Department of Labor, p. 124.

41. PL 101–648, 101st Congress.

42. PL 104–320, Section 11.

Chapter Four

1. For a study of the growth of the federal common law of labor-management arbitration, see Cooper, L., and Nolan, D., *Labor*

Arbitration: A Coursebook, St. Paul, Minn.: West, 1994, chapter 6.

2. Section 302, 29 USCA, § 185.

3. Cox, A., "Grievance Arbitration in the Federal Courts," *Harvard Law Review*, 1954, 67(591), 605–606.

4. *Textile Workers Union v. Lincoln Mills*, 353 US 448, 77 S Ct 912 (1957).

5. *United Steelworkers of America v. Warrior and Gulf Navigation Co.*, 363 US 574, 80 S Ct 1347 (1960).

6. Shulman, H., "Reason, Contract and Law in Labor Relations," *Harvard Law Review*, 1955, 68, 999–1024.

7. *United Steelworkers of America v. American Manufacturing Co.*, 363 US 564, 80 S Ct 1343 (1960).

8. *United Steelworkers of America v. Enterprise Wheel and Car Corp.*, 363 US 593, 80 S Ct 1358 (1960).

9. *Collyer Insulated Wire*, 192 NLRB 837 (1971).

10. *Spielberg Mfg. Co.*, 112 NLRB 1080 (1955).

11. *Olin Corporation*, 268 NLRB 573 (1984).

12. Meltzer, B., "Ruminations About Ideology, Law and Labor Arbitration," *Proceedings of the Twentieth Annual Meeting of the National Academy of Arbitrators* 1967, pp. 1–20.

13. Howlett, R., "The Arbitrator, the NLRB and the Courts," *Proceedings of the Twentieth Annual Meeting of the National Academy of Arbitrators*, 1967, pp. 67–110.

14. *Alexander v. Gardner-Denver Co.*, 415 US 36, 94 S Ct 1011 (1974).

15. 9 USC, §§ 1–16 (1994).

16. *Gilmer v. Interstate/Johnson Lane Corp.*, 500 US 20, 111 S Ct 1647 (1991).

17. 9 USC, §§ 1, (1994).

18. 45 ABA Rep 293 (1922).

19. Subcommittee Hearings of the Committee of the Judiciary on S. 4213 and S. 4214, 67th Congress, 4th Session, Jan. 31, 1923, p. 9.

20. *Willis v. Dean Witter Reynolds*, in 948 F 2nd 305, 311 6th Cir 1991 (Quoting hearings in S. 4213 and S. 4214 before the Subcommittee on the Judiciary, 67th Congress, 4th Session (1923), p. 9.

21. *Willis v. Dean Witter Reynolds*, letter from Hoover to Senator Thomas Sterling in hearings.

22. *Tenney Engineering v. United Electrical Workers*, 207 F 2nd 450 (3rd Cir 1953).

23. For a comprehensive examination of *Gilmer* and its environment, see "Developments in the Law—Employment Discrimination," *Harvard Law Review*, 1996, 109(7), 1670–1692.

24. *Asplundh Tree Expert Co. v. Bates* 71 F 3rd 592 (6th Cir 1995).

25. CA–93–51–D decided March 12, 1996, *Daily Labor Report*, Washington, D.C.: Bureau of National Affairs, March 15, 1996, p. E–1.

26. *Prudential Insurance Company v. Lai*, 42 F 3rd 1299 (9th Cir 1994) cert. denied 116 S Ct 61 (1995).

27. *Williams v. Cigna Financial Advisors*, 56 F 3rd 656 (5th Cir 1995).

28. Motions on Alternative Dispute Resolution Adopted by the EEOC, April 25, 1995.

29. *EEOC v. River Oaks Imaging and Diagnostic*, No H–95–755, 1995 WL 264003 (SD Texas Apr. 19, 1995).

30. *Great Western Bank*, Case No 12–CA–16886 and *Bentley's Luggage Corp.*, Case No 12–CA–16658, 1995. Also see William B. Gould IV, "Alternative Dispute Resolution and the National Labor Relations Board: Some Ruminations About Emerging Legal Issues, Jose Canseco, and Gertrude Stein." *Daily Labor Report*, Washington, D.C.: Bureau of National Affairs, Apr. 10, 1997, pp. 3–4.

31. Report issued May 1996 by task force chaired by Governor James J. Florio and Mayor Jerry Abramson; Jonathan Brock, Executive Director.

32. "National Academy of Arbitrators' Statements and Guide-

lines," *Daily Labor Report*, Washington, D.C.: Bureau of National Affairs, May 29, 1997, pp. E—1—2. The NAA issued "Guidelines on Arbitration of Statutory Claims Under Employer-Promulgated Systems."

33. *Alford v. Dean Witter Reynolds*, 939 F 2nd 228 (5th Cir 1991).

34. *Metz v. Merrill, Lynch, Pierce, Fenner and Smith, Inc.*, 39 F 3rd 1482 (10th Cir 1994).

35. *Pritzker v. Merrill, Lynch, Pierce, Fenner and Smith, Inc.*, 7 F 3rd 1110 (3rd Cir 1993).

36. Bompey, S., *Use of Arbitration and Other ADR Programs: A Reasonable Alternative to Resolve Employment Disputes*, Paper presented at ABA Annual Meeting, Aug. 4–7, 1996.

37. See Hope B. Eastman and David H. Rothenstein, "The Fate of Mandatory Employment Arbitration Amidst Growing Opposition: A Call for Common Ground," *Employment Relations Law Journal*, 1995, 20(595).

38. Reuben, R., "Investors' Attorneys Find Task Force Report Faulty," *ABA Journal*, Apr. 1996, pp. 40–41.

Chapter Five

1. General Accounting Office, *Employment Discrimination: Most Private-Sector Employers Use Alternative Dispute Resolution*, July 1995. Also see Bingham, L. B. "Emerging Due Process Concerns in Employment Arbitration: A Look at Actual Cases," *Labor Law Journal*, Feb. 1996, pp. 108–127; and "Is there a Bias in Arbitration of Nonunion Employment Disputes? An Analysis of Actual Cases and Outcomes," *International Journal of Conflict Management*, Oct. 1995, pp. 369–386.

2. *Resolution, Brown & Root Dispute Resolution Program*. The program provides four options: open door policy, conference, mediation, and arbitration.

3. Sept. 23, 1994, "Memorandum to All Site Managers," p. 1.

4. "ITT Headquarters Mediation and Arbitration Policy," issued Jan. 25, 1994, with covering letter stating in part: "We are implementing the attached ITT Corporation Headquarters Mediation and Arbitration Policy Effective February 1, 1994.

You should review the Policy carefully. Finally complete the acknowledgement form enclosed with the Policy and return it to the ITT Headquarters Human Resources Department by no later than March 1, 1994."

5. Oct. 1, 1995; sent to "All Associates," with a cover letter from the Director of Human Resources including the following: "By continuing your employment after October 1, 1995, the effective date of the Plan, you agree to follow the terms of the Plan."

6. From the company with a place at bottom of the memorandum for employee's signature and date.

7. Sept. 23, 1994 "Memorandum to All Site Managers," containing the following caveat: "Because the attached Arbitration Agreement is written in legalese it may be difficult for supervisors and/or employees to understand."

8. Oct. 31, 1994 letter to "Dear Astra Member" attached to the Aug. 24, 1994 original announcement containing the following: "This arbitration procedure applies automatically to all new employees hired on or after July 1, 1994 and to all employees who were on probation effective July 1, 1994. All employees hired before July 1, 1994 who wish to receive any future allocations to the Astra Profit Sharing Program must sign the Agreement."

9. USWEST, Inc. "Non-Qualified Stock Option Agreement," Dec. 1994, sec. 6, p. 2.

10. Bentley's Luggage Corp., "Employee Commitment to the Program," June 7, 1994.

11. "ITT Corporation Policy," Feb. 1, 1994, p. 2.

12. A.F.M. Services, Inc. (Archer) Agreement form, Sept. 7, 1994, paragraph 2, which also exempts from arbitration workers' compensation, unemployment insurance benefits, and claims relating to employee evaluations, bonuses, merit increases, layoffs, and wage claims of any kind.

13. Sec. 8 of the agreement form described in Note 12.

14. "EPRP Arbitration Procedure," effective January 1, 1993.

15. *Resolution, Brown & Root Dispute Resolution Program*, Questions and Answers, p. 17.

16. "Archer Agreement," sec. 4, p. 1.
17. "Archer Agreement," sec. 7, p. 1.
18. "EPRP Arbitration Procedure."
19. "Travelers Group Employment Arbitration Policy," Apr. 1996, sec. 6, p. 83.
20. *Resolution, Brown & Root Dispute Resolution Program*, p. 12.
21. "ITT Plan," p. 3.
22. River Oaks Imaging and Diagnostic Center, "Memorandum of December 16, 1994 to All Employees, Mutual Agreement to Arbitrate Claims Form," p. 3.
23. "Hughes EPRP Arbitration Procedure," p. 2.
24. Bridgestone/Firestone Inc., "Employee Dispute Resolution Plan," effective Oct. 1, 1995, p. 9.
25. "ITT Plan," page 3.
26. "Traveler's Group Employment Arbitration Policy," Apr. 1996, sec. 24, p. 86.
27. "Hughes EPRP Administration Procedure," p. 2.
28. AstraUSA, Inc., "Employment Dispute Resolution Arbitration Agreement," issued Aug. 24, 1994, sec. 2.
29. "Hughes EPRP Arbitration Procedure," p. 2.
30. Bridgestone/Firestone Inc., "Employee Dispute Resolution Plan," sec. 6, p. 4.
31. "Archer Agreement," sec. 9, p. 2.
32. "River Oaks Arbitration Agreement," p. 2.
33. "ITT Corporation Headquarters Mediation and Arbitration Policy," p. 3.
34. *Resolution, Brown & Root Dispute Resolution Program*, Questions and Answers, p. 17.
35. "Archer Agreement," Sept. 23, 1994, sec. 4 and 5, p. 2.
36. "Bentley Arbitration Form," June 7, 1994.
37. "Travelers Group Employment Arbitration Policy," sec. 20B, pp. 85–86.
38. Astra plan, sec. 11b.
39. "Primerica Employment Arbitration Policy," Sept. 1992, sec. 20B.

40. USWEST, Inc., "Non-Qualified Stock Option Agreement," Dec. 1994, sec. 6.

41. American Arbitration Association, *National Rules for the Resolution of Employment Disputes, Arbitration and Mediation Rules, Effective June 1, 1996*. See further revision effective June 1, 1997. *Daily Labor Report*, Washington, D.C.: Bureau of National Affairs, May 28, 1997, pp. E—17—26. Also see American Arbitration Association, *Guide for Employment Arbitrators*.

42. "When It's Time to Do Battle with Your Company," *Business Week*, Feb. 10, 1997, pp. 130–131.

Chapter Six

1. Howell, W., *Years of My Youth*, New York: Harper and Brothers, 1916, p. 107: "I have never regretted reading a first volume of Blackstone through, or not going on to the second; his frank declaration that the law was a jealous mistress and would brook no divided love, was upon reflection quite enough for one whose heart was given to a different muse."

2. J.A.M.S./Endispute, "Six Principles of Neutrality and Fairness for Employment Dispute Resolution Practice," 1996.

3. *Resolution, Brown & Root Dispute Resolution Program*, effective June 15, 1993, p. 5.

4. For a discussion of payment of arbitrators' fees, see *Clinton Cole v. Burns International Security Services, et al.*, F 3rd (D.C. Cir 1997).

Chapter Seven

1. Except for the discussion of Massachusetts in Chapter Eight, the individual states are generally outside the scope of this volume. Readers interested in the detail and variety of state regulation of labor markets may wish to explore "State Labor and Employment Laws Enacted in 1996," *Daily Labor Report*, Washington, D.C.: Bureau of National Affairs, Feb. 4, 1997.

2. PL 101–552, as amended by PL 102–354.

3. PL 104–320.

4. Section 571(3).

5. Federal Mediation and Conciliation Service, *Alternative Dispute Resolution Services to Government*, Washington D.C.: Federal Mediation and Conciliation Service, 1997.

6. PL 101–552, Sections 575–581.

7. Administrative Conference of the United States, *Toward Improved Agency Dispute Resolution*, Feb. 1995, pp. 43–44.

8. Article II, Section 2, clause 2:

[The President] shall nominate, and by and with the advice and consent of the Senate, shall appoint Ambassadors, other public Ministers and Consuls, Judges of the supreme court, and other officers of the United States, whose appointments are not herein otherwise provided for, and which shall be established by law: but the Congress may by law vest the appointment of such inferior officers, as they think proper, in the President alone, in the courts of law, or in the heads of departments.

9. U.S. Department of Justice, Office of Legal Counsel, "Constitutional Limitations on Federal Government Participation in Binding Arbitration," Sept. 7, 1995.

10. Executive Order 12988—Civil Justice Reform, *Federal Register*, Feb. 7, 1996, 61(26), 4729–4734.

11. For a listing of some of the major statutes, see U.S. General Accounting Office, *Workplace Regulation: Information on Selected Employer and Union Experiences*, vols. I and II, Washington, D.C., June 1994. This study surveys 26 major laws and one executive order out of the more than 180 laws administered by the Labor Department alone.

12. PL 104–121. Also see Department of Labor, Office of Small Business Programs, *User's Guide to the Small Business Regulatory Fairness Act of 1996 and Related Laws*, Jan. 15, 1997.

13. For a tabular comparison of some of the features of a few employment statutes, see Commission on the Future of Worker-Management Relations, *Fact Finding Report*, May 1994, pp. 132–133.

14. Commission on the Future of Worker-Management Relations, *Report and Recommendations*, Dec. 1994, p. 33.

15. For investigative staff data, see Commission on the Future of Worker-Management Relations, *Report and Recommendations*, Dec. 1994, p. 54.

16. See Schuyler, *A Cost Analysis of the Department of Labor's Philadelphia ADR Pilot Project*.

17. See Moscowitz, E., and Van Bourg, V., "Carve-Outs and the Privatization of Workers' Compensation in Collective Bargaining Agreements," *Syracuse Law Review*, 1995, 46(1), 1–60. This article is critical of some features of these collectively bargained plans. For an analysis of the evolution of the California Industrial Accident Commission, administering workers' compensation, see Nonet, P., *Administrative Justice, Advocacy and Change in a Government Agency*, New York: Russell Sage Foundation, 1969.

18. *Logan International Airport Terminal Area Construction Labor Agreement between O'Brien-Kreitzberg Associates, Inc., and Metropolitan District Building and Construction Trades Council*, June 17, 1993, p. 49.

19. California Division of Workers' Compensation, *The Construction Carve-Out Program: A Report of Activities in Calendar Year 1995*, July 1996.

20. See USDL: 96–376, Sept. 11, 1996. Trained agency specialists, nonlawyers, settle routine penalty appeals, freeing attorneys to work on more complex cases. In the first year these specialists handled 26 percent of the cases in which mine operators contested agency civil penalties. The program received Vice President Gore's "Hammer Award" for reinvention of government.

21. *Federal Register*, Feb. 12, 1997, pp. 11734–11748; *Daily Labor Report*, Washington, D.C.: Bureau of National Affairs, Feb. 13, pp. E17–23.

22. *Daily Labor Report*, Special Report, Washington, D.C.: Bureau of National Affairs, Jan. 17, 1997, p. S–19.

23. Federal Labor Relations Authority, *FLRA NEWS*, Jan. 26, 1996, pp. 104–196.

24. Federal Mediation and Conciliation Service, *Alternative Dispute Resolution Services,* Washington, D.C., 1996; also see statement of Deputy Director Wilma B. Liebman before the Committee on the Judiciary, Subcommittee on Commercial and Administrative Law, U.S. House of Representatives, June 27, 1996, and *Forty-Eighth Annual Report* for the fiscal year 1995, Washington, D. C., 1997, pp. 43–50.

Chapter Eight

1. Chapter 568 of the Laws of 1989, effective January 1, 1990, created an experimental program, to expire June 30, 1994, that authorized parties to proceedings before the New York State Division of Human Rights who alleged unlawful discrimination under the Human Rights Law (Sec 296 et seq., Executive Law), to elect to arbitrate their case in lieu of proceeding further before the division.
2. *Report to the Governor and Legislature by the Human Rights Arbitration Advisory Committee,* Mar. 31, 1994, Pauline Kinsella, Chair, 37 pp.
3. The full text is available in *Employment Discrimination Report,* Vol. 6, Washington, D.C.: Bureau of National Affairs, Feb. 28, 1996, pp. 258–261.
4. MCAD RFP 96–1, Feb. 15, 1996.

Chapter Nine

1. These size data refer to 1992. See Commission on the Future of Worker-Management Relations, *Fact-Finding Report,* May 1994, pp. 8–9. The data on firm size are for workplaces covered by state unemployment insurance laws and thus exclude some firms, self-employed workers, railroad employees, agricultural workers, and some others.
2. See *Small Business Handbook: Laws, Regulations and Technical Assistance Services,* Washington, D.C.: U.S. Department of Labor, 1993.

3. Davis, S., Haltiwanger, J., and Schuh, S., *Job Creation and Destruction*, Cambridge, Mass.: MIT Press, 1996, p. 1.

4. Davis, Haltiwanger, and Schuh, *Job Creation and Destruction*, p. 57.

5. Dunlop, J., *Industrial Relations Systems*, 2nd ed., Boston, Mass.: Harvard Business School Press, 1993, pp. 43–130.

6. See Commission on the Future of Worker-Management Relations, *Report and Recommendations*, Dec. 1994, pp. 1–5.

7. Executive Order 12988—Civil Justice Reform, *Federal Register*, Feb. 7, 1996, 61(26), 11734–11748.

8. As noted in Chapter Seven, a Department of Justice memorandum of Sept. 7, 1995 states, "there are no constitutional impediments preventing federal agencies from voluntarily engaging in the use of binding arbitration."

9. *Federal Contracts Report*, Vol. 65, Washington, D.C.: Bureau of National Affairs, pp. 460–461.

10. *From Red Tape to Results*, Appendix A, p. 146. (See Chapter One, note 45.)

11. See Harter, P., "Dispute Resolution and Administrative Law: The History, Needs, and Future of a Complex Relationship," *Villanova Law Review*, 1983–84, 29(6), 1393–1419.

12. "External Third-Party Review of Significant Employee Concerns: The Joint Cooperative Council for Hanford Disputes," Working Papers in Public Policy Analysis and Management, Graduate School of Public Affairs, University of Washington, 1993. Jonathan Brock had a significant role in the development and administration of the Joint Council.

13. Bingham, G., *Resolving Environmental Disputes: A Decade of Experiences*, Washington, D.C.: Conservation Foundation, 1986. Significant early developments include the National Coal Policy Project. See Murray, F., *Where We Agree: Report of the National Coal Policy Project*, vols. 1 and 2, Boulder, Colo.: Westview Press, 1978. John T. Dunlop served as facilitator at an early session on July 9–10, 1976, at the Airlie Conference Center outside Washington, D.C.

14. *Resolve*, 1996, 27, 16.

15. See presentation to the Commission on the Future of Worker-Management Relations, Aug. 26, 1993, Richard A. Coughlin, P.E., Executive Director, 1150 Connecticut Avenue, N.W., Suite 600, Washington, D.C., 20036–4104. In 1996, Allan D. Silberman was DART's Executive Director.

16. *Engineering News-Record*, Special Advertising Section, Oct. 19, 1992, pp. 8, 10.

17. The first awards were made on May 13, 1993, in Washington, D.C.

18. Smith, R., *Alternative Dispute Resolution for Financial Institutions*, Deerfield, Ill.: Clark Boardman Callaghan, 1995.

19. Kraut, W., "Domestic Relations Advocacy—Is there a Better Alternative?" *Villanova Law Review*, 1983–84, 29(6), 1379–1392.

20. See Dunlop, J., *The Management of Labor Unions: Decision Making with Historical Constraints*, San Francisco: New Lexington Press, 1990, pp. 3–23.

21. General Accounting Office, *Employment Discrimination: Most Private-Sector Employees Use Alternative Dispute Resolution*, July 1995, pp. 3, 29.

22. Commission on the Future of Worker-Management Relations, *Fact-Finding Report*, May 1994, pp. 120, 136.

23. *Report of the General Counsel, January to September, 1995*, National Labor Relations Board, Washington, D.C., Feb. 16, 1996, (R–2126), pp. 4–9; *Daily Labor Report*, Washington, D.C.: Bureau of National Affairs, Feb. 23, 1996, pp. E4–6.

24. See *Keeler Brass*, 317 NLRB 110, July 14, 1995. In his concurring opinion, Chairman Gould stated, "I would find no domination provided employees controlled the structure and function of the Committee and their participation was voluntary" (p. 1119). Also see speech of Chairman Gould of Feb. 29, 1996, Indianapolis, Indiana, "Beyond 'Them and Us' Litigation: The Clinton Board's Administrative Reforms and Decisions Promoting Labor-Management Cooperation."

25. *Working Together for Public Service*, p. 81.

26. *Working Together for Public Service*, p. 83.

27. Sections 576 and 577.

28. Commission on the Future of Worker-Management Relations, *Report and Recommendations*, Dec. 1994, pp. 29–30.

29. See Zimny, M., "Arbitration of Statutory Employment Dispute Under Collective Bargaining Agreements," in *Contemporary Issues in Labor and Employment Law, Proceedings of the New York University 49th Annual Conference on Labor*, 1997; Estreicher, S., "Essay, Freedom of Contract and Labor Law Reform: Opening Up the Possibilities for Value-Added Unionism," *New York University Law Review*, 1996, 71(3), 827–849. But see the opinion of Chief Judge Posner in *Vincent L. Pryner v. Tractor Supply Company*, 7th Circuit, March 20, 1997, *Daily Labor Report*, Washington, D.C.: Bureau of National Affairs, March 25, 1997, pp. E—1—7.

30. The FMCS "developed a policy of furnishing panels for non-union situations. This policy evolved as a result of requests we received under the Freedom of Information Act." See letter of Feb. 15, 1995 from Eileen B. Hoffman, General Counsel of the agency, to Mr. James J. Perry, Appalachian Power Company. The FMCS has revised its rules on arbitration, 29CFR Part 1404. *Daily Labor Report*, Washington, D.C.: Bureau of National Affairs, March 13, 1997, pp. E—17—25.

Index